John Fraser

The humorous chap-books of Scotland

John Fraser
The humorous chap-books of Scotland
ISBN/EAN: 9783743341838
Manufactured in Europe, USA, Canada, Australia, Japa
Cover: Foto ©ninafisch / pixelio.de

Manufactured and distributed by brebook publishing software (www.brebook.com)

John Fraser

The humorous chap-books of Scotland

TO

ALEXANDER SCOTT, Esquire,

GREENOCK, SCOTLAND.

(*Mæcenas, atavis edite regibus, &c.*)

I.

Go, little book, across the throbbing seas,
   To bear from me and mine,
Some humble tribute of the love we owe
    A friend of "auld lang syne."

II.

No more this hand may "tak' a haud o' his,"
   No more these eyes may trace
The kindly smile, the unaffected look,
    Of that familiar face.

III.

Ah! nevermore those hours so full of light,
   Of well-remembered talks,
By lovely Barrochan's romantic braes
    And ivy-shaded walks!

IV.

But hearts may touch where hands can never meet,
   And mine goes out to home;
To dear old Scotland yearning hands I stretch
    Across the salt sea-foam.

CONTENTS.

CHAPTER I.

INTRODUCTORY REMARKS.

SECTION
1. What are Chap-books?
2. The objects and limits of this book.
3. Previous writings on the subject.
4. The character and value of chap-books.
5. Political aspects of Scotland in the eighteenth century.
6. Social aspects.
7. Want of roads and conveyances.
8. Insecurity of life.
9. Popular superstitions.
10. Severity of the penal code.
11. Tyranny of the Kirk Session.
12. Tyranny in the domestic circle.
13. One-sided administration of law.
14. Intemperance of the age.

SECTION

6. The 'Glasgow bell-man' in the olden time.—Dougal, after a fierce struggle, is appointed the "skellat bellman" of Glasgow.
7. Dougal's writings.
8. His death and Elegy thereon.
9. His minor poetical effusions.—"John Highlandman's Remarks on Glasgow."—"Turnimspike."
10. His personal character.
11. His position as a Scottish Humorist.

CHAPTER IV.

GENERAL CLASSIFICATION OF SUBJECT.

I.—Dramatic Sketches.

SECTION

1. "Jockie and Maggie's Courtship."—Critical remarks.—Curious Scotch custom of 'bedding.'
2. "The Coalman's Courtship."—Critical remarks.
3. "The Art of Courtship."

SECTION

4. "Silly Tam" *alias* "Simple John."—Other versions of same.
5. "History of the Haverel Wives."
6. Brief notice of some poetical chap-books.
7. "A Diverting Courtship."
8. "The Pleasures of Matrimony."—Other versions of same.

CHAPTER V.

II.—Simple Prose Narratives.

Introductory Remarks :—The heroes of vulgar romance.—The Scottish 'natural.'—Character of the Fools of Roadside Fiction.—General classification.

SECTION

1. "George Buchanan."—Different versions of same.—Analysis of the History.—Critical remarks.—Connection between Scholarship and Sorcery.—The wise fools of history.—The original of the George Buchanan of fiction.—Source of the various stories.—Brief notice of the English chap-book entitled "Tarlton's Jests."

SECTION

2. "Lothian Tom."—Analysis of same.—Critical remarks.—Lothian Tom's English prototype.—Brief notice of the English chap-book entitled "The Merry Conceits of Tom Long, the Carrier."—The 'Toms' of fiction.—John Franky, the English fool.

CHAPTER VI.

II.—Simple Prose Narratives.—Continued.

SECTION

1. (3.) "John Cheap, the Chapman."—Analysis of his exploits.—Critical remarks.
2. (4.) *a.* "Leper, the Tailor."—*b.* "The Grand Solemnity of the Tailor's Funeral."
3. (5.) "John Falkirk's Jokes."
4. (6.) "John Falkirk's Carriches."—Critical remarks.—Immorality of the lower classes in Scotland last century.
5. (7.) "Paddy from Cork."
6. (8.) "History of Buchaven; or, Wise Willie and Witty Eppy."

General resume of the preceding Chapters.
Concluding remarks.

THE HUMOROUS CHAP-BOOKS

OF

SCOTLAND.

CHAPTER I.

§ 1. *What are Chap-books?*
§ 2. *The objects and limits of this book.*
§ 3. *Previous writings on the subject.*
§ 4. *The character and value of chap-books.*
§ 5. *Political aspects of Scotland in the Eighteenth Century.*
§ 6. *Social aspects.*
§ 7. *Want of roads and conveyances.*
§ 8. *Insecurity of life.*
§ 9. *Popular superstitions.*
§ 10. *Severity of the penal code.*
§ 11. *Tyranny of the Kirk Session.*
§ 12. *Tyranny in the domestic circle.*
§ 13. *One-sided administration of law.*
§ 14. *Intemperance of the age.*
§ 15. *Popular games.*
§ 16. *General features.*

§ 1. It is easier to say what a chap-book is, than to define what it is not. As M. Charles Nisard, in his account of the popular literature of France, remarks of the " almanachs,"—"*Il ne manque pas de gens aujourd'hui qui pensent vous embarrasser en vous demandant qui n'a pas son journal? Ils vous embarrasseraient bien davantage s'ils demandaient qui n'a pas son almanach?"* So it may be asked, what are not chap-books? *Chambers's Encyclopædia* defines them as "a variety of old and scarce tracts of a homely kind, which at one time formed the only popular literature. In the trade of the bookseller they are distinguishable from the ordinary products of the press by their inferior paper and typography, and are reputed to have been sold by chapmen or peddlers." This, however, is not nearly comprehensive enough, including but a very small portion of the literature embraced under the class 'chap:' for chap-books vary greatly in shape, price, and character; from the half-penny villainously printed sheet of paper or broadsheet, containing the last dying speech and confession of Nichol Mushet, the murderer, to the neatly bound and fairly printed "History of the Rebellion in 1745," consisting of some 200 pages, and illustrated with diagrams and a likeness of the author. In short, 'chap-book' was the name given to almost every species of publication that was hawked round the country districts of Scotland last century,—

including broadsides of all kinds; humorous sketches, sacred and profane; political and sectarian squibs; histories, romantic and narrative; jest-books and manuals of instruction in dancing, cookery, charms, and the interpretation of dreams: ranging in price from a farthing to a six-pence and a shilling each. Originally, the word had a more limited signification; the earliest chap-books being nearly uniform in size and price. Each volume consisted of a twenty-four-page single sheet, duodecimo, execrably coarse in texture, dirty gray or whity-brown in colour, illustrated by one or more rough woodcuts, and printed in a rude and unfinished style of typography. In size and shape they were identical with their modern representatives, which are still issued in large numbers under the name of 'penny histories,' and are sold at country fairs and gatherings in Britain by travelling packmen. The prefix 'chap' originally meant 'to cheap or cheapen,' as in the word 'cheapening-place,' meaning a market-place,—hence the English Cheapside and Eastcheap. 'Chapman' is the designation given to those peddlers, or, as they were often called, 'flying' or 'itinerant' stationers, who at one time were the only merchants in rural districts; and the literature, which they carried nicely assorted in their packs in little pigeon-holes, was called chap-books.

§ 2. It is not our intention to treat of chap-books in the larger signification of the word. That would necessitate the introduction of several chapters on love-songs, ballads, party squibs, and miscellaneous tracts, which have been discussed repeatedly by many eminent men; and to the information already accumulated regarding which no one, who did not devote the greater part of his life to the work, could hope to add any thing new. While, therefore, it will be necessary to refer incidentally to these forms of literature, these chapters will be devoted to a consideration of those humorous penny histories, and sketches—mostly of local origin, and consisting generally of twenty-four pages—which may be said to have sprung into existence toward the middle of last century, and to which we must turn for the fullest and truest expression of the habits, humours, and every-day life of the Scottish commonalty during that period.

§ 3. Motherwell, the Paisley poet, writing forty-eight years ago, says, " in truth it is no exaggeration when we state, that he who desires to acquire a thorough knowledge of low Scottish life, vulgar manners, national characteristics, and popular jokes, must devote his days and nights to the study of *John Cheap, the chapman; Leper, the tailor; Paddy from Cork; the Whole Proceedings of Jockie and Maggie's Courtship; Janet Clinker's Orations; Simple John and his twelve Misfortunes*, etc." Yet how few modern readers, even in Scotland, are familiar with so much as the titles of the tracts just enumerated? But a few years ago, *John Cheap* and his brethren were distributed broadcast over Scotland by countless flying stationers, and sold in thousands at every fair, hamlet and country gathering north of the Tweed; yet at this hour their very names are forgotten, and the original or unexpurgated editions are to be found only on the shelves of antiquarians and old-booksellers

As early as 1824, Motherwell was unable to make a complete collection of them; and in his eloquent introduction to "Scottish Songs," published in 1825, Allan Cunningham laments "that those little copies have vanished before the influence of a more fleeting literature." Abridged versions of most of them are still in circulation, but the veritable narratives, which formed the intellectual food and amusement of the common people for nearly a hundred years, are now all but passed away and forgotten. There are many reasons why this is to be regretted; not the least cogent being that no record of the history and character of this kind of literature remains, to throw light upon the manners and tastes of a bygone age. More attention is paid to the subject in France. In 1852 the Imperial Government of that country appointed a Commission to examine into the character and influence of French chap-books; and two years later the secretary to the Commissioners published a semi-official work, in two handsome and beautifully illustrated volumes, entitled, "Histoire des Livres Populaires ou de la Littérature du Colportage, *depuis le XVe siècle jusqu'à l'établissement de la Commission d' examen des livres du colportage*, (30 *novembre*, 1852,) par M. Charles Nisard, Secrétaire-adjoint de la Commission. Paris, Librairie D'Amyot, Editeur, 8, rue de la Paix, mdccclix." In England, again, Dr. J. O. Halliwell-Phillips, to whom students of literature are so deeply indebted, has done something to rescue from oblivion the 'littérature du colportage' of that country, and more than one antiquarian has performed a like service for that of Ireland. But Scottish chap-books, superior in every respect to kindred productions in England, Ireland, and France, have been altogether ignored. This is the more to be wondered at when it is remembered, that Sir Walter Scott was so impressed with the importance of the subject, that he entertained serious intentions of undertaking some such work as that here desiderated. Motherwell, too, cherished a like design, and went so far as to make a fair collection of the necessary material; but all that he has left is a few brief notes in a local journal of which he was editor—the "Paisley Magazine for 1824." In the article referred to, Motherwell reveals one secret of his failure. After explaining, with a groan, that he had at one time possessed a fair assortment of the original editions of many popular penny histories, the enraged editor goes on to say, "but some unprincipled scoundrel has relieved us of that treasure. There are a number of infamous creatures, who acquire large libraries and curious things by borrowing books they never mean to return, and some not unfrequently slide a volume into their pocket at the very moment you are fool enough to busy yourself in showing them some nice typographic gem, or bibliographic rarity. These dishonest and heartless villains ought to be cut above the breath whenever they cross the threshold. They deserve no more courtesy than was of old vouchsafed to witches, under bond and indenture to the devil." This failure on the part both of Scott and Motherwell, undoubtedly the two most competent men of their age for the task, is the more unfortunate because they have left so few behind them able and willing to undertake the duty. With the exception of Dr. Laing, of Edinburgh, whose hands are already full, and to whom Scotland owes so much for his splendid and unselfish labours in the cause of her early literature, there is no well-known writer from whom we should naturally expect a work of the kind. It was mainly the consciousness of this fact, and the knowledge that each fresh delay but made more difficult the task of investigation and research, that impelled the writer to move in the matter, and throw together such facts as he succeeded in gleaning, in connection with a subject of which so little is, and so much ought to be, known.

Besides the brief and not quite accurate paper in the *Paisley Magazine*, above mentioned, and a few lines in *Chambers's Journal* and *Encyclopædia* there is absolutely nothing in the language on the subject of Scottish chap-books. The late Dr. Strang of Glasgow, in his entertaining gossip about Glasgow clubs, remarks, in a foot-note to a brief notice of Dougal Graham,—" A history of the vulgar literature of Scotland has been long and is unquestionably still a desideratum, for certainly nothing could tend to throw so much light on the manners and tastes of the great body of the people as such a work." Twenty years have elapsed since the publication of "Glasgow and its Clubs," and up to this writing no attempt has been made to fill the long-felt gap in the national literature of Scotland, which so moved the sympathies of Sir Walter Scott, Motherwell, and Dr. Strang.

§ 4. Professed history is too frequently confined to a record of the more striking results of the passions and virtues of eminent personages, and the transactions of a nation in its collective capacity—to the neglect of the nice shades of moral and social progress, the private life of the *dramatis personæ*, and, of course, of the great public—whose mode of living, thoughts, loves, sorrows, joys, hopes, and fears were, until lately, considered to be unworthy the notice of the historian. And yet what is thought, and said, and felt is as real history, and as important to be known, as that which is visibly done by man to man. It is impossible thoroughly to understand the history of Scotland, or the character of her people during the last century, without studying these vulgar, but graphic and intensely Scottish, productions under review. For many years they constituted the chief and universal literature of old and young, among the lower and agricultural middle classes, throughout the lowlands; and in them we have reflected the mind, superstitions, customs, and language of the people who read them, more accurately and vividly than in the stately pages of Robertson or of Hume. In every point of view the Chapbook is full of interest. It guides us to the manners and customs of an age gone by; it reveals to us the popular mind and feelings more surely and sharply than the most elaborate treatise; its incidents are strongly felt and forcibly described; its images, those which Nature suggests, not the combinations of refined art: and the customs, adventures, and superstitions narrated, are clothed in the rude, simple, energetic and nervous language of a half-unlettered people.

They originated in the necessities of an age just sufficiently educated to feel the want of cheap literature, and cut off by the puritanical and traditional austerities of the clergy and people, from popular amusements and sports. They filled the place now occupied by cheap concerts, lectures, newspapers, and the shoal of serial publications which cater for the public taste. But, apart from their historical value, they claim for themselves a distinct and unique place in literature, for their intrinsic and literary merits. It has been too much the fashion to regard rough, idyllic sketches like *Jockie and Maggie's Courtship*, as rude, illiterate productions, possessing a considerable share of humour, but interesting chiefly for their grossness and rarity. It will be shown by-and-by that they are much more and much other than this; that the most characteristic of them are written with extraordinary vigour, humour, and dramatic skill: and are entitled to be ranked with such classical masterpieces as the humorous narratives in the *Canterbury Tales*. But before proceeding to trace their history and growth, and to criticise in detail their merits and defects, it will be necessary briefly to sketch the political, literary, and domestic features of the age, on which the chap-books throw so strong and truthful a light.

§ 5. On the 15th of November, 1688—day ever memorable in the annals of Britain—William, Prince of Orange, landed with his army in England, to take possession of the throne made vacant by that weak-headed bigot, James: and on the eleventh of April, 1689, William and Mary were crowned at London, and proclaimed at Edinburgh. Three months later, Prelacy was officially abolished, and the Presbyterian form of Church government which now exists established in its stead. At the same time, the parochial system of schools, concerning which several tentative enactments had been previously passed, was finally settled. These, and other measures, went some way to consolidate the hold of the new sovereigns on the affections of the Scottish nation; and, if they had been left to work out their results in peace, would probably have put an end to the disaffection and broils which, for many years afterward, kept the country in a continual state of fermentation. But, unfortunately, the new Government soon turned its back on Scotland; intent only on the depression of France, and the overthrow of the Roman Catholic interest in Europe. This might have passed unnoticed by the public, if it had not been for the stupendous bungling and wickedness of William's subordinates, which brought about the tragedy of Glencoe, on the 13th of February, 1692. Scarcely had the nation recovered from the shock occasioned by this atrocity, when it was a second time overwhelmed, by the disastrous Darien expedition; the collapse of which was mainly owing to the unjust and short-sighted jealousy and opposition of the English Government. A great famine, which laid waste the country about the same time, aggravated the already embittered feelings of the people; which were further intensified by the ratification of the Act of Union in February, 1707, (Queen Anne being then on the throne,) in direct and flagrant opposition to the expressed wishes of the whole Scottish nation. This, which eventually proved an incalculable blessing to both countries, was at first a fertile source of jealousy, heart-burning, and discontent. To make bad worse, several statutes were passed immediately afterwards that pressed severely and specially on the Scots; and every thing was done that could exasperate, and left undone that might conciliate, their affections. All these things incensed a people naturally proud; making a revolution possible, and turning the eyes not only of Jacobites and Catholics, but of Pope-detesting Presbyterians, to the exiled house of Stuart. An event soon occurred to precipitate the impending crisis. On the 1st of August, 1714, Queen Anne died, her husband having predeceased her by twelve years, and the Elector of Hanover was called to the throne, under the title of George the First. The new King inaugurated his accession to power by unceremoniously turning the Tories out of doors, and replacing them with Whigs; which so enraged some of the already disaffected noblemen, that the Earl of Mar, with one or two others, hurried north to his Scotch estates, and raised the standard of revolt in the name of the Pretender, on the 6th of September, 1715. Scotland must have been terribly provoked before the country could rise, as it did, in large numbers, to place a Catholic on the throne. From the first, however, misfortune dogged the footsteps of the rebels; and when, on December 22d, the ill-fated son of James VII. landed at Peterhead, he found his cause at the point of collapsing. In little more than two months, owing to general imbecility and want of spirit, the ruin of the Pretender's hopes was completed; and, on February 7th, the fast dwindling army of rebels was disbanded at Aberdeen. About this time, the good effects produced by the Union on the commerce of the country began to be realized in the lowlands, particularly in Glasgow; which, being favorably situated with respect to the American and West-Indian colonies, was fast losing its character of a small episcopal town, and assuming that of a great manufacturing capital. In the commercial centres of the South the old feeling of disaffection and resentment was on the wane; and Glasgow was among the first to raise and dispatch a contingent to aid Argyll in crushing the rebellion. But Glencoe is not in Lanarkshire, and north of the Grampians the popular feeling still ran in another and quite opposite direction. As late almost as 1800, Scotland may be said to have consisted of two great divisions, inhabited respectively by people of different race, language, and manners. The larger in surface, a range of mountain pastures, was held by Celts; possessing all the peculiarities of that people unmodified, with many of the common characteristics of pastoral and half-savage life,—faithful, brave, hardy; patient of suffering, but constitutionally indolent; incapable of sustained exertion: and superstitiously averse from change. They had lived hitherto regardless of all law but the will of their chiefs,—ignorant of all patriotism beyond a passionate attachment to their native glens.

Across the 'Highland Line' was a people differing in all respects from their northern neighbours—frugal, and patient of toil; cautious yet not cowardly, nor devoid of enterprise; sober-minded; not generally imaginative, but with a vein of romance capable of being excited to the highest enthusiasm: and tenacious of purpose to obstinacy. In spite of local circumstances, this people had early taken a part in the intellectual struggle of Europe. A national system of schools had spread the benefit of education through all classes; and, although by no means bustling politicians, yet in questions affecting their liberty or religion, no people could be more energetic, or more splendidly lavish of their goods and lives.

With |their Highland countrymen they had no sympathy; regarding them as aliens in blood and language, and little better than lawless and dangerous barbarians. The recollection of the ill-fated Darien expedition, and the misgovernment of William and Mary, had begun to fade from the minds of men engaged in active business and prosperous pursuits; and the good results of the Union were beginning to make themselves seen, in rapidly increasing towns, growing intelligence and comfort, security of life, and commercial activity. These beneficial influences had not yet pierced into the mountainous recesses of the North, where still, as ever, the name of Englishman was synonymous with injustice and oppression.

On the wild and hardy highlanders the claims of hereditary loyalty had made a deep impression, which their own wrongs, and the military glories of Montrose and Dundee, had combined to deepen. Thus, while south of the Firth of Forth and Tay, George I. held sway over a peaceful, industrious, and well-disposed people,—north of that line his rule was utterly and fiercely disowned, by rebellious and warlike clans; nearly as different from their southern brethren in manners, ideas, dress, and language, as if they had been born west of the Alleghanies. To this state of matters the Government were not sufficiently alive; and, whether from supineness or ignorance, they allowed the feeling of isolation and disaffection, which had spread through the northren countries, to smoulder unheeded amid the glens; while the exiled Stuarts used every means to keep it alive, until such time as it suited them to fan it into the flame of open rebellion. Thus, while the lowlanders, who were mostly Whigs or Presbyterians, were experiencing the benefits of the Union, in the rapid multiplication of their factories, schools, and shipping—their ruder neighbours, who were chiefly Jacobites or Episcopalians and Catholics, were as ready in 1745, as they had been thirty years before, to declare themselves for the Stuart line. An opportunity at length offered, and on the 22d of June, 1745, Prince Charles Edward, the Pretender's son, landed on the west coast with a retinue of seven persons; preparatory to raising the standard of revolt at Glenfinnan, on the 19th of August following. Into the details of the young Pretender's daring but ill-starred enterprise it is unnecessary to enter. It is sufficient to say, that the same cruel fate which had never ceased to dog the royal line of Stuart, from the assassination of James the First, continued to pursue the brave but misguided Charles, whose hopes were forever overthrown and crushed on the field of Culloden, 16th April, 1746.

To Scotland, the immediate consequences of the rebellion were temporary oppression by the English troops, and the ruin of many noble families. Its remoter consequences were of a different character. The attention of the Government was now most effectually roused to the condition of the Highlands; and decisive measures were at once adopted to eradicate all seeds of disloyalty, by a summary dissolution of the old patriarchal system. For this purpose, in 1747, the hereditary jurisdictions were purchased or wrested from the heads of clans; a new act was passed for the more effectual disarmament of the Highlanders; and another, which however was repealed soon after as inexpedient and oppressive, prohibiting the wearing of tartan clothes. The tenure of ward-holdings was abolished; and legislative provision was made for the regular administration of justice by the King's judges throughout North Britain. The rebellion did good, too, by setting forever at rest the Stuart claims, and permitting the people to settle down in tranquil industry under the Brunswick sway. An immense impulse was in this way given to the national prosperity. The whole system of trade, husbandry, and manufactures, which had hitherto proceeded by slow degrees, began to make rapid advances; and the increased communication between the Highlands, Lowlands, and England broke down, in some measure, the barriers which the ignorance and prejudices of centuries had helped to rear,—so that the movement was not isolated or confined to the large towns, but was the outcome of the simultaneous exertion of the united strength of the whole nation.

The commencement of the reign of George III., in 1760, marks another era of great improvement in the condition of Scotland. Through the wise influence and advice of the Earl of Bute—whom, shortly after his accession to the throne, George placed at the head of affairs—Scotland obtained for the first time that share of general consideration and public employment to which it was entitled. All animosities respecting succession were now at rest; the people were experiencing the good effects of trade and industry; and with wealth came refinement of manners, and a more general diffusion of the comforts of life. It is unnecessary to pursue this branch of inquiry further. The above rude outline is merely meant to serve as a reminder, to refresh the memory of the reader, and prepare him for the right understanding of what follows.

§ 6. The eighteenth century was eminently a transition age; so are all periods more or less, but in this case the transition from a lower to a much higher level was unprecedentedly rapid. Hand labour was giving place to machinery; ignorance and coarseness to knowledge and light; old landmarks were being obliterated; old institutions assailed. The paths trodden by the footsteps of ages were broken up, and the prejudices and customs—legacies of a thousand years—were passing away never to return. Although printing had been established in Edinburgh and Glasgow in the end of the 16th and beginning of the 17th centuries respectively, and had crossed the Grampians in 1622, books were still too rare, expensive, and learned, to be widely circulated or read. The educational condition of the people was indeed deplorable. In schools the universal text-book was the Catechism; and the library of a well-to-do farmer consisted of that treatise, a Bible, and a collection of penny histories and broadsides. Comparatively few in the humbler ranks could read or write; and the chief intellectual food of the people, in the earlier part of the century, was the songs and ballads recited and sung by peasants or peddlers, who took the place of the old minstrels, whom the Reformation had swept away with kindred "follies." From 1567 may be dated the publication of broadsides, which then began to be issued in considerable numbers from the Edinburgh press. It is doubtful how far they were circulated among the common people. The probability is that they were not popularly read until well on in the 17th century. In 1644, the Rev. Zacchary Boyd complained to the General Assembly that "their schools and country were stained, yea pestered, with idle books, and their children fed on fables, love-songs, baudry ballads, heathen husks, youth's poison." The year 1696 saw the establishment of the Presbyterian Church, and the system of parochial schools; the beneficial results of which began after some years to show themselves in a general improvement of the national tone, and a growing desire for intellectual food. Increased facilities for education and increased security of property, co-operated powerfully to soften and modify the national character, and divert energies, hitherto misspent or misdirected, into channels of morality and industrial pursuits. But it was long before these good results became vulgarly apparent. Many circumstances combined to retard and hinder the national progress. Of such were the political fermentation in the north; the want of means of communication throughout the country; the inequality of the laws, and the maladministration of justice; and the superstition and ignorance of the people generally. On these points Sir Archibald Grant, a Highland laird of the time under review, gives clear and decisive evidence. According to this authority, husbandry and manufactures were in very low esteem for many years after the Union.

So long as the feudal system continued in force, land was looked upon rather as a source of power than of revenue. Even in years of abundance, all its produce was consumed on the spot, being obtained by the unskilled and desultory labours of men, whose only object was to secure the means of subsistence, and whose regular employment was war. These retainers lived in wretched one-roomed hovels, crowded around the castle of their chief. The arable land in the neighbourhood was kept constantly under corn crops; and beyond it, a large tract was occupied in common, chiefly in the pasturage of cattle. Sir Archibald informs us, in his reminiscences, that turnips in fields, for cattle, were wondered at; wheat was confined to East-Lothian; inclosures were few, and planting was very little; roads were excessively rare, and, without exception, bad, there being no one to repair them; while north of the Tay there were no coaches, chariots, or chaises, and even carts were almost unknown. A friend of Sir Archibald, one Colonel Middleton, was the first person who employed carts or waggons at Aberdeen; and these two were the first to possess hay north of the Forth. Table and body-linen were coarse in texture, and seldom shifted; movable necks and sleeves being worn by the upper classes. Wooden, mud, and thatched houses existed in large numbers within the gates in Edinburgh, Glasgow, and Aberdeen; while without, few houses of any better kind were to be found. Tyranny reigned everywhere. Nobles and chiefs were tyrants; so were the clergy and the privy council, and the bailies and magistrates: and there was no such thing as fixed property or liberty. Grant's account of his own paternal estate in Aberdeenshire, then not behind the greater part of Scotland, is important.

"By the indulgence of a very worthy father, I was allowed, when very young, to begin to inclose, and plant, and provide, and prepare nurseries. At the time (1716), there was not one acre on the whole estate inclosed, nor any timber upon it, but a few elm, sycamore, and ash, about a small kitchen garden adjoining to the house, and some straggling trees at some of the farm-yards, with a small copsewood not inclosed, and dwarfish, and browsed by sheep and cattle. All the farms ill-disposed and mixed; different persons having alternate ridges; not one wheel-carriage on the estate, nor indeed any one road that would allow it, and the rent about £600 sterling per annum; grain and services converted to money. The house was an old castle, with battlements, and six different roofs, of various heights and directions, confusedly and inconveniently combined, and all rotten; with two wings, more modern, of two stories only; the half of the windows of the higher rising above the roofs; with granaries, stables, and houses, for all cattle and the vermin attending them, close adjoining; and with the heath and moor reaching in angles or gushets to the gate, and much heath near, and what land near that was in culture belonged to the farms, by which *their cattle and dung were always at the door.* The whole land raised and uneven, and full of stones, many of them very large, of a hard iron quality, and all the ridges crooked in shape of an S, and very high and full of noxious weeds, and poor, being worn out by culture, without proper manure or tillage. Much of the land and moor near the house poor and boggy; the rivulet that runs before the house in pits and shallow streams, often varying channels, with banks always ragged and broken. The people poor, ignorant, and slothful, and ingrained enemies to planting, inclosing, or any improvements or cleanness; no keeping of sheep, or cattle, or roads; farm-houses, and even corn-mills, and manse and school, all *poor, dirty huts, pulled in pieces for manure, or fell of themselves, almost each alternate year.*"

§ 7. This account of the carriages and roads is confirmed by all the chap-books of last century, in not one of which is a coach, cart, or waggon once alluded to. People who went on journeys used horses, and travellers were divided into two classes—equestrian and pedestrian. In *Jockie and Maggie's Courtship*, composed and published after 1750, Jockie and his mother pay a visit to a friend who resides in the neighbourhood. So in the morning, " the brose being done, an' a' things ready, Jock halters the black mare, lays on the sunks an' a covering—fine furniture for a country wife. Jockie mounts an', his mither behind him, trots awa' till coming down the brae aboon John Davie's well, the auld beast being unferry o' the feet, she foundered before, the girth an' curple brake, Jockie tumbled o'er her lugs, an' his mither out o'er him, in the well wi' a slunge." In the same way when Maggie ran for Uncle Rabby, and Uncle Rabby sent for Sandy the Souter of Seggyhole, "The Souter saddled his mare, an' Uncle Rabby got off at a gallop on his grey powney."

To make matters worse, the few roads which did exist were little better than beaten tracks, made rugged and at times impassable by swollen torrents, or mountain thieves and caterans. Regular communication was all but unknown, and in 1763 there was only one stage-coach between Scotland and London. This conveyance set out from Edinburgh once a month, and took from fifteen to eighteen days to get over the ground. In 1678, an attempt was made to run a coach between Edinburgh and Glasgow, but it fell through for want of support. Sixty-five years later, in 1743, the magistrates of both cities tried to induce one John Walker to start one, to travel twice a week from either town, the Glasgow officials guaranteeing him the sale of two hundred tickets yearly in their own city. But the scheme was thought too risky, and fell through. In 1749, a respectable citizen from the Trongate, named John McIlquham, went on a journey to London, and was ever afterward called 'London John.' Amusing evidence to the same effect is furnished by Lord Lovat's account of a journey from Inverness to Edinburgh in 1740.

"I came off on Wednesday, the 30th of July, from my own house, dined at your sister's, and did not halt at Inverness, but came all night to Corribrough, with Evan Baillie and Duncan Fraser; and my chariot did very well. I brought my wheelwright with me the length of the Avemore, in case of accidents, and there I parted with him, because he declared that my chariot would go safe enough to London; but I was not eight miles from the place, when, on the plain road, the axletree of the hind wheels broke in two, so that my girls were forced to go on bare horses behind footmen, and I was obliged to ride myself, though I was very tender and the day very cold. I came with that equipage to Ruthven late at night, and my chariot was pulled there by a force of men, where I got an English wheelwright and a smith, who wrought two days mending my chariot; and, after paying very dear for their work, and for my quarters two nights, I was not gone four miles from Ruthven, when it broke again, so that I was in a miserable condition till I came to Dalnakeardach, where my honest landlord, Charles McGlassian, told me that the Duke of Athol had two as good workmen at Blair as were in the kingdom, and that I would get my chariot as well mended there as at London. Accordingly, I went there and stayed a night, and got my chariot very well mended by a good wright and a good smith. I thought then I was pretty secure till I came to this place. I was storm-stayed two days at Castle Drummond by the most tempestuous weather of wind and rain that I ever remember to see. The Dutchess of Perth and Lady Mary Drummond were excessively kind and civil to my daughters and to me; and sent their chamberlain to conduct me to Dunblaine, who happened to be very useful to us that day; for I was not three miles gone from Castle Drummond, when the axletree of my fore-wheels broke in two in the midst of the hill, betwixt Drummond and the Bridge of Erdock, and we were forced to sit in the hill with a boisterous day, till chamberlain Drummond was so kind as to go down to the Strath, and bring wrights, and carts, and smiths, to our assistance, who dragged us to the plain, where we were forced to stay five or six hours, till there was a new axletree made; so that it was dark night before we came to Dunblaine, which is but eight miles from Castle Drummond; and we were all much fatigued. The next day we came to Lithgow, and the day after that, we arrived here; so that we were twelve days on our journey by our misfortunes, which was seven days more than ordinary."

Even in Glasgow and Edinburgh, private carriages were exceedingly rare, the fashionable mode of conveyance being the sedan-chair. In some verses, entitled *John Highlandman's Remarks on Glasgow,* by Dougal Graham, author of the Metrical History of the Rebellion of '45, already mentioned, and whose name will occur frequently in the course of this book, we have a humorous description of one of these chairs—

" And tere I saw another mattam,
   Into a tarry sack,
And twa poor mans be carry her,
   Wi' rapes about him's neck—

She pe sae fu' o' fauity,
   As no gang on the grun',
Put twa poor mans pe carry her,
   In a barrow covered abune'."

§ 8. This want of roads and means of communication, necessarily isolated districts and communities from the rest of the country; and, in the Highlands especially, proved a fertile source of evil. Cattle-lifting, blackmail, and highway robberies abounded; and where there was no security there could not be any deep attachment to the reigning government. The inhabitants of the Highlands generally, and of the adjacent country, were grievously oppressed by gangs of lawless thieves and robbers from the remote north, who stole and openly carried off their horses and cows; and as Badenoch, in particular, lay near the seats of those ruffians, great numbers of its inhabitants were reduced to beggary. Several attempts were made to obviate these evils, but without success, until Macpherson, of Cluny, in the summer of 1744, undertook — on consideration of being paid a certain sum to be raised by general subscription— to rid the district of thieves, to recover stolen property, and to become liable for the losses sustained by any one who contributed to the relief fund. This was, in fact, a revised edition of the black-mail system pursued by Rob Roy, who, however, stole more cattle than he recovered. In Cluny's hands it proved completely successful: so much so, that when a certain clergyman began a sermon on the heinous nature of the crime of theft, an old Highlander in the audience interrupted him with the remark, that he need not say anything on that subject, as

Cluny with his broadsword had done more to check thieving, than all the ministers put together could do by their sermons. This general insecurity was not confined to Scotland, but extended to all parts of the Kingdom, and furnished material for the large collection of cheap literature, devoted to deeds of violence, bloodshed and highway robberies. Among the best known of these works are,—*McPherson's Rant, Rob Roy, Jack Shepherd, Dick Turpin, The Gentleman Robber, George Barnwell, David Haggart, The Negro Robber, Jack Mansong, The Female Robber, The Irish Assassin, The Bloody Gardener, Redmond O'Hanlan, McPherson, Fleemy, Balf, Gilder Roy, Donald McDonald, and Moll Flanders.*

§ 9. Hand-in-hand with the want of cheap, intelligent literature, went that lusty handmaiden of ignorance—Superstition. An unbeliever in charms, dreams, fortune-telling, witchcraft, and the visible activity of elves, brownies, witches, warlocks, and the devil, with other superhuman and demoniacal agencies, was accounted little better than an atheist. Fishermen purchased a fair wind and a heavy 'take' from some sham Æolus; maids and mistresses consulted the travelling conjuror as to the time and results of their marriage; and if a child fell sick, or a cow's milk failed, or the horse took the 'balts,' or the good man had an unusually severe headache after a 'spree,'—it was attributed to the 'evil eye.' The clicking of the death-watch, the rites of Hallowe'en and New Year, and the 'candle spail,' were regarded with reverence and fear; and every woman in the land read her fortune in her tea-cup.

Thus, in *The Coalman's Courtship*, when Sawny comes home drunk, and is put to bed, pale and haggard, his mother cries,—

"Wa Sawny man, what's come o'er thee now? Thou's gotten skaith; some auld wife's bewitched ye!"

So, too, *Janet Clinker's Orations* is full of superstitious allusions. Two old gossips, Maggy and Janet, are discussing the affairs of the parish, when the former expresses her surprise, that the "deils dinna flee on the minister whan he flytes and miscas them sae;" and asks her friend "if she thinks they hear him?" On which Janet:

"Ay, they hear and see too, they are neither blind nor bleer'd; but ay whan ye speak o' them name the day, cry its Wednesday thro' a' the warld, and there's nae fear o' you"——— "Indeed, they say there's black deils and white anes o' them, humel anes and horn'd anes, the very witches is ha'f deils whan they're living, and hale anes whan they're dead. The brownies are ha'f dogs, ha'f deils, a' rough but the mouth, seeks nae claise, ae man's meat will sare them and they'll do ten men's wark in ae night;* for it's hobgoblins, fairies and elfs, that shoots folk's beasts to death, and no hole to be seen in the skin o' them. H'ard ye no tell o' the twa Highland wives? how the tane cried, "Ochon, Shenet, my cow is shot!" "Hoch," quo she, "wha shot her?" "Deed, it was the Deil." "Och, Shenet, we'll a' be shot whan the de'il has gotten a gun!"

In *The Pleasures of Matrimony* the young lady's maid visits a conjuror, to discover whether a certain gallant is in love with her mistress; and the gallant himself goes to the same place on a similar errand. So, again, the incident in the *History of John Cheap the Chapman*, where John, on

---

* This reminds one of Milton's drudging goblin, whose shadowy flail by night would thrash the corn
   "That ten day-labourers could not end."

being refused bread and milk by the inhospitable farmer's wife, knots three or four long straws, and, muttering some gibberish, pretends to bewitch the cows in the byre; handing over the kirn, butter and milk, sap and substance, without and within, to the tender mercies of the enemy of mankind.

In the Highlands, the faculty of second-sight was invariably and implicitly believed in, and every parish boasted its seer or seers, of both sexes. The vision came upon the seer without premonition. If, in the morning, the prediction was expected to be fulfilled within a few hours; if, at noon, not for days. Was a woman seen standing at a man's left hand?—the vision presaged the marriage of the pair; and if several women stood in a row beside a man, the one next him would be his first wife, and the second nearest his second, the third his third, and so on. Sometimes, a spectre or browny intervened to produce the phenomenon. At one time almost every family in Zetland had a browny, to whom they gave sacrifice for his service. When they churned their milk, a portion of it was sprinkled on every corner or house for the use of the spirit; and when they brewed, some of the wort was poured through a hole in what was called the 'Browny's Stone' as a sacrificial offering. Certain stacks of corn, too, were called 'Browny's Stacks,' from off which, though they were unbound with straw-ropes, the greatest storm of wind was unable to blow any straw. Predictions of death formed a large class of cases of second-sight. The event was usually indicated by the subject of vision appearing in a shroud, and the higher the vestment rose on the figure, the nearer was the event. So late as 1763 an educated man published a treatise in defence of the delusion, and even at the present day in the remoter parts of the Highlands second-sight is implicitly believed in.

Allusion has been made to witchcraft, the history of which occupies a large and ugly place in the annals of Scotland. "While Presbyterianism," writes the late Robert Chambers, " of the puritanic type reigned uncontrolled between 1640 and 1651, witches were tortured into confession and savagely burnt, in vast numbers; the clergy not merely concurring, but taking a lead in the proceedings. During the Cromwell ascendancy, English squeamishness greatly impeded justice in this department, to the no small dissatisfaction of the more zealous. On the Restoration, the liberated energies of the native powers fell furiously on, and got the land in a year or two pretty well cleared of, those vexatious old women who had been allowed to accumulate during the past decade. From 1662 to the Revolution, prosecutions for witchcraft were comparatively rare, and, however cruel the government might be towards its own opponents, it must be acknowledged to have introduced and acted consistently upon rules to some extent enlightened and humane with regard to witches—namely, that there should be no torture to extort confession, and no conviction without fair probation. * * * * * For a few years after the Revolution, the subject rested in the quiescence which had fallen upon it some years before. But at length the General Assembly began to see how necessary it was to look after witches and charmers, and some salutary admonitions about these offenders were from time to time issued. The office of Lord Advocate or public prosecutor, had now fallen into the hands of Sir James Stewart of Goodtress, a person who shared in the highest convictions of the religious party at present in power, including reverence for the plain meaning of the text, 'thou shalt not suffer a witch to live.' The consequence was, that the reign of William III. became a new Witch Period in Scotland, and one involving many notable cases." The wretched creatures were tortured on the rack, drowned in ponds, burnt at the stake, and starved or beaten to death. Most frequently, when convicted, the victim was gagged with a broad piece of iron, called the 'witch's bridle,' which was forced into the mouth so as to press down the tongue. The head was then fixed in an open case, to which was attached a chain by which to rivet the body to the stake. Every little district and village had its 'witch-detector,'—an infamous impostor who pretended to be able to discover witches from an examination of the moles upon their bodies, these being thought to be nips given at birth by Satan, and insensible to pain. If, on the mole being pierced with a long needle, made for the purpose, the suspected person showing signs of being pained, he was at once found guilty and burnt, and the result of the examination depended entirely on the amount of the fee with which the detector had been bribed; for the 'brod,' or needle, was so contrived that the operator, by touching a spring, could make the steel retire into its sheath. In England, it is estimated, that more than 30,000 'witches' were burnt, while the number of those who perished in Scotland is incalculable. At one sitting alone, of the Parliament in Edinburgh, upwards of 600 persons were indicted for witchcraft. The charges generally related to some alleged practising against the health of men, or cattle, or the growth of crops; and there is a remarkable uniformity in the description of the sickness caused by witches, which seems to indicate the prevalence of violent fever and ague. To cure, was as dangerous to cause, disease; and the imputations were often childishly absurd. Against one woman it was proved, that one night, while her husband was lying in bed, and she was dressing, a cat came and, after sitting upon him, and crying 'wallawa!,' worried one of her kittens: whereupon the goodman slew it, immediately after which his horse and dog went mad. This damning evidence against the woman was further confirmed by the fact that her children were all 'quick-ganging devils;' for one day an evil spirit, disguised as a magpie, chased the youngest out of the house, and tried to peck her eyes out.

It is impossible, in short, to imagine any transaction of life into which sorcery might not enter, and advantage was taken of the superstition, by unscrupulous persons, to gratify private passions and spleen, or to accomplish other unholy ends. Among the forms most frequently assumed by evil spirits were those of the cat, hare and dog. The devil appeared to his servants, sometimes as an old grey-bearded man, with a white gown and a 'thrummy' hat; sometimes as a black man, a lamb, a calf, or a horse: and, at others, in the shape of a black beast, which rose out of the ground in the midst of its worshippers, and waxed larger by degrees. He loved to officiate as chairman at the midnight revels of witches and warlocks, and to promote the harmony of the evening by extemporising infernal ditties. On one occasion, according to Sinclair, the veracious author of *Satan's Invisible World Discovered,* the fiend, disguised as a young maiden, most ravishingly beautiful, appeared to certain of the sons of men, and sang a song of his own composition, which became suddenly very popular. In the Spalding Club *Miscellany* (1841-42), there is preserved a curious account of " The debursements made by the comptar, at command and by virtue of the Provost, Bailies, and Council, in the burning and sustentation of the witches:

	£.	s.	d.
Imprimis for burying Suppak, who died in prison	0	6	8
Item for trailing Manteith through the street of the town in a cart, who hanged herself in prison, and for cart hire and burying her	0	10	0
Jonet Wischart and Issbell Cocker.			

Item for twenty loads of peat to burn them	0	40	0
Item for a boll of coals	0	23	0
Item for four tar-barrels	0	26	8
Item for fire and iron barrels	0	16	8
Item *for a stake and dressing it*	0	16	0
Item for four fathom of tows	0	4	0
Item for carrying the peats, coals, and barrels to the Hill	0	13	4
Item for *Jon Justice* [Jack Ketch] for their execution	0	13	4

Thomas Leis.

Item, the 23d of Feb., for peats, tar-barrels, fire and coals, to burn the said Thomas, and to Jon Justice for his fee in executing him	3	13	4

The last witch executed in Scotland was a poor Highland woman, a native of the parish of Loth, in Sutherlandshire, who was burnt in a pitch-barrel at Dornoch, for having transformed her daughter into a pony, and had her shod by the devil. This took place in June, 1722; but the Statutes against witchcraft were not repealed till 1750. So late as 1851, one Andrew Dawson, in practice as a veterinary surgeon somewhere in the region of the Grampians, was had up before the Kirk Session on a charge of sorcery, and summarily excommunicated for having cured certain diseases by means of 'chucky stanes.' The universality of the belief in fortune-telling, dreams, ghostly visitations, and the like, is attested by the number and character of the chap-books which treat of the supernatural. Among the best known of these are *Visits to the World of Spirits*, *The Prophecies of Thomas a' Rhymer, Peden, &c., &c.*, *The Spaewife*, *The Golden Dreamer*, *Professor George Sinclair's Satan's Invisible World Discovered*, fortune-telling books of every description, and mole and dream interpreters in endless variety; besides such comparatively recent works as *Buonaparte's Book of Fate*, and the like.

It was not till the beginning of the present century that this great fabric of superstition was materially shaken. In *John Cheap the Chapman* and similar sketches, written and published after 1750, there are many indications that a great change was passing over the popular mind. *John Cheap* himself, although he frightens the goodwife into hospitality by making believe to bewitch her cattle, makes haste to escape from the neighbourhood in case the trick may be discovered. He has, indeed, a wise contempt for such quackery, which intelligence on the part of a drunken peddler shows how the belief in charms and witchcraft, was rapidly dying out, or, at least, becoming greatly modified. That it has quite perished even now, however, cannot be affirmed; for to this day there are hundreds who think it unlucky to travel on a Friday; or to be born or married on certain days; or to go to fish if they are met by a black cat in the morning; and who feel uncomfortable at dinner if they are helped to salt; or their neighbour, having spilled it, has neglected to throw a portion of it over his shoulder. To this day, too, the herring-fishers of Lochfyneside have a lucky and an unlucky method of doing everything. It is considered, for instance, unlucky to turn back for anything; or to give a bit of fire to one's neighbour when barking nets. Neither will a fisherman dare put a net on board his boat on the first night of the season unless the tide is at flood; or go to sea on the same occasion if a woman do not first grace his boat with her presence, and either smile, or drink success to his fishing. An Ardrishaig shipbuilder would shudder at the thought of launching a boat against the sun, or in a line not parallel with the course of that luminary. Another superstition is that herring always desert the neighbourhood of land which has been manured with their dead fellows; and believers in this fancy point conclusively to Shicidig, a small village in the North of Scotland, where, on one occasion, years ago, a heavy fishing was had, and there being no salt at hand, the herring were used to manure the soil. Since that day, it is said, no member of the herring tribe has ever visited that shore. There are still one or two old men who, when hauling in their nets with a good 'shot' of 'maskit' herring, or, to use the technical provincialism, a 'good strag,' always sprinkle a 'puckle salt' on the fish, in order to counteract the baneful influence of some possible evil eye that may be on them. Allan Cunningham, in a passage of remarkable beauty, written in 1825, bewails the vanishing of these dreams of superstitious belief.

A 4

A poetical and imaginative power, he writes, nursed these old beliefs in spite of their education and the light which learning shed; while their southern neighbours, having less imaginative power, and much less knowledge, dismissed them as idle and unprofitable encumbrances. Much of the richness of the illustration, much of the poetical strength of expression, has left us: and what was accounted the fittest food for the Muse is charmed away from her lips by the magic-wand of adventure, invention, and discovery. To a shepherd's way of life, poetry may be supposed to have little to add, since his whole existence seems poetical; yet, when the arrows of the elves, and the spells of the witches, were broken or destroyed, the poetical part of sheep-surgery departed also: he now consults the receipt-book, and seeks no longer to avert or cure the evil which has fallen on his flock, by the poetry of charms or conjurations. The mariner, when he spreads his sail for a foreign shore, no longer purchases a favourable wind and a prosperous voyage from the witches of Lapland or Galloway;

and though he whistles for a breeze when the sea is calm, he does so more through custom than from the hope of awakening the sleeping wind. The fisherman, when he dips his nets in the water, thinks not now of augmenting his draught of fish by warbling to his victims a charmed rhyme; and the cowherd, when he drives his cattle to the pasture, has forgot of late to regulate their movements, and protect them from the spells of witches, with a rod of rowan-tree. *A horse-shoe is no longer nailed above the stable-door, as a charm against the entrance of mischievous beings; nor is an ox's head buried under the barn threshold, to ensure the coming of the corn unblighted to the flail. The maid dreads no more the influence of evil eyes over her gathering of cream, as the churn staff ascends and descends amid the fragrant element; and the

---

* This statement can hardly be correct, as, even now, after the lapse of nearly half a century, the horse-shoe is to be found nailed to the doors of barns, stables, and smithies in the Western Highlands of Scotand, although it may be that much of the ancient meaning has fled; and the persons who nail them on hardly know why they do it, unless it be that their fathers did so before them.

matron, as she bars her door at night, summons no more

Saint Bride and her brat,

and all other powers, in whose might her ancestors had belief, to protect her and hers from all manner of fiends and shapes in the service of Satan. These and many other rural superstitions of a poetical nature, have melted away before the thaw of knowledge. When the peasant stood on the hill-top, and looked to earth and sky as the sun sank, to discover the promise of to-morrow, he composed something like the rudiments of poetry as he remarked the colours of the clouds, and the amplified or decreased appearance of the hills, and deduced from the varied scene before him the certainty of sunshine or rain. He sits at home now and consults his almanack. When time was computed by the sun's shadow, or by the evening light, a shepherd, as he gazed on the stars and moon, composed the poem while he pondered out the hour; the bughting star and the northern wain, and the plough, are all names fitted for rustic poetry; but they have slipped out of conversation now that a watch has usurped their office. Men had their lucky days on which they transacted business; a sailor was unwilling to weigh anchor on a Friday; and a family was sure to be overwhelmed with calamity and misfortune, had the head of the house chanced to marry in May. Two magpies on the roof of a dwelling house were ominous of a funeral in one county, and of a wedding in another; a hare hirpling before a youth as he was on the way to his love, during the twilight, has made him turn pale, and induced him to break his tryste; while a shower of rain on a bridal procession has gone nearer to snatch the bride from the bridegroom's arms, than all the address and cunning of his rivals. I have known men set down a corpse, and wait till a cloud interposed between them and the sun, before depositing it in the earth. Such a superstitious feeling is still recorded in English rhyme:

> Happy is the bride that the sun shines on,
> And happy is the corse that the rain rains on.

These and innumerable other remains of a

curious and primitive people have been current in many men's memories; and as they contain the very elements of poetry, there can be little doubt that poetry has suffered by their loss, and that man is becoming more of a machine—an instrument capable of cultivating a given quantity of ground—a spinning-jenny for preparing thread—a kind of military engine covered with plumes and scarlet, for demolishing towns and destroying the human species.

§ 10. Another feature of the age was the extreme severity of its penal enactments. There was never a Glasgow Ayre closed its sittings that several wretches were not doomed to execution for crimes, or rather misdemeanors, which now-a-days would be amply punished by a brief imprisonment. Men and women were drummed out of the city and banished from the burgh for slight offences, or cat-of-nine-tailed through the public thoroughfares at the back of a cart, to be pelted with mud and refuse by a brutal, unsympathising rabble. The last woman who suffered in this way was flogged along Argyll street, Glasgow, in 1793.

The following extracts from the *Glasgow Mercury* speak for themselves:

"Thursday, July 30th, 1778. On Monday, Barbara Barber was tried before the Magistrates of this City for keeping a bawdy house. She was sentenced to remain in prison till Wednesday the 12th of August next, and then to stand on the Tolbooth stair-head with a label on her breast, having these words,— '*For keeping a notorious bawdy house;*' and afterwards to be banished from the city and liberties for seven years, under the usual certification."

"Glasgow, December 24th, 1778. By sentence of the Magistrates, Catharine Buchanan and Sarah McDougal are to stand on the Tolbooth stair-head, bareheaded, on Wednesday the 30th of December, with a label on their breasts, '*I stand here for theft and reset of theft*'; and afterwards to be sent to the house of correction for two months, and Catharine Buchanan to be banished from the town for seven years. The process was carried out at the expense of the protecting society."

A few years earlier, Catharine Buchanan and Sarah McDougal would have been hanged; a few years later, imprisoned for seven or ten days.

§ 11. The same spirit of harshness and severity prevailed everywhere, and in no quarter more prominently than in the Church. For nearly two centuries the jurisdiction of the Kirk Session had been submitted to without a grumble. Its judgments were binding as the edicts of the Council of Nice; irrevocable as the statutes of the Medes. Everywhere the influence of the Church reigned supreme. Its authority penetrated to the most secret places of domestic life, invading the sanctity of the kitchen, and seriously curtailing the dimensions of the wardrobe. If a person absented himself from one diet of divine service on Sunday, he was fined in three shillings and four pence; if he went to any other kirk than his own, he was mulcted in twice that sum. One or two magistrates were told off to watch at the church doors, to take a note of the absentees; while others were appointed to report on such of the members as disgraced themselves by drunkenness. Does not *Leper*, the tailor, inform us how two 'zealous civileers,' one Sunday afternoon, invaded the kitchen, and carried away his 'kail pot,' on the ground that he should be at Kirk, and had no right to be cooking during divine service? The fines imposed for breaking the Sabbath, besides making public repentance, graduated, according to the repetition, or the gravity of the offence, from six shillings and eight pence to £6 Scots.

A curious instance of the religious superstition of the times was the fact, that fast days were thought to be more sacred than the Sabbath, and consequently any desecration of them was punished with even more severity; the lowest fine being forty shillings for the first, eighty for the second, and one hundred and twenty for the third offence. Persons were also prohibited from public walking on Sunday, and children from appearing in the street on the same day. Profane swearers were fined a shilling an oath; adulterers were ducked in the river; prostitutes were publicly whipped, and banished for life; 'change-houses' were searched by the elders every Saturday night, with the view of 'dilating' drinkers; wife-beaters were compelled to 'ride the stang;' and scolds had to stand in the church aisle in sack cloth, and make public confession of their evil tongue. The stringency of these regulations regarding the observance of the Sabbath, and the sin of incontinency, naturally gave the clerical conclaves abundant matter for jurisdiction, and led to many and serious evils: so much so, that as the Kirk increased in severity, the people sank deeper in vice; and the most gross immorality, intemperance, superstition, ignorance, and child murder, were accompanied by a pharasaical observance of religious rites, and an austerity that refused to countenance Maypole dances, Robin Hood games, mysteries, plays, and every kind of popular amusement and sport,—including 'penny weddings' and country 'fairs.' *Leper*, the tailor, thought it no sin to get most beastly drunk on Sunday, but was filled with horror at the idea of shaving on that day; *John Cheap* compelled the elder to give him lodging and food, by threatening to tell 'the minister' if he refused; and other chap-books of the period teem with references to the terrible judgments of the Kirk Session. The 'Jug' and the 'Cutty Stool' were the two most prominent articles of ecclesiastical furniture, in the 16th, 17th and 18th centuries; and the dread which they inspired was a fertile source of infanticide and other evils. The

Records of the Books of Presbyteries and Sessions contain abundant proof of the rapid increase of illegitimacy which succeeded the Reformation. Towards the end of the 17th century, it was declared in the legislature that there were frequent murders of innocent infants, whose mothers concealed their pregnancy; and it was accordingly enacted that women found guilty of this sort of secrecy, and whose babes were dead or missing, should be held as guilty of murder, and punished accordingly. In other words, Society, by treating female frailty with puritanic severity, held out the most powerful temptation to unfortunate women to conceal the fact of their pregnancy, and the consequence of their sin; and then, on merely negative evidence, punished with death the very crimes which it had itself induced. But, terrible as this act was, it did not avail to make women brave the severity of that social punishment which stood on the other side. It had, accordingly, many victims, and furnished the incident on which, as everyone knows, the *Heart of Midlothian* turns. As might be expected in an age so harsh, and careful of the outsides of the platters, laws were passed, ecclesiastical and civil, to restrain excess in personal expenditure. At one period work-people were restricted on 'week-days' to clothes of grey and white, and on holidays to light blue, green, and red; while their wives' 'curches' were ordered to be home made, not exceeding forty-pence the ell; and no woman was allowed to go to Kirk or market with her face veiled, under pain of 'escheat' or forfeiture of the curch. After the Revolution, the discipline of the church abated somewhat of its rigour; but its lay-officer or Kirk-treasurer, was still a very formidable person. The poems of Ramsay, and the chap-books generally, are full of allusions to the terrible powers, not only of the Kirk-treasurer himself, but of his 'man' or servant. In a parody by the younger Ramsay on the *Integer Vitæ* of Horace, this personage is set forth as the analogue of the Sabine wolf:

"For but last Monday, walking at noon-day,
  Conning a ditty, to divert my Betty,
    By me that sour Turk (I not frighted) our Kirk-
      Treasurer's man passed.

And sure more horrid monster in the Torrid
Zone cannot be found, sir, though for snakes re-
nowned, sir;
Nor does Czar Peter's empire boast such creatures,
Of bears the wet-nurse."

Burt, in his *Letters*, goes so far as to assert that the Kirk-treasurer employed spies to report upon private individuals, so that people lay at the mercy of villains who were ready to forswear themselves for sixpence. Card and dice playing in taverns, with drinking and desecration of Sunday, were the crimes which gave most employment to these active emissaries. Especially was their anxiety strong about Sabbath observance. It seemed, says Burt, as if the Scotch recognized no other virtue. People would startle more at the humming or whistling of a tune on a Sunday, than if anybody should tell them you had ruined a family. Innumerable extracts might be given from the vulgar literature of the age, bearing out the above remarks, but the following may serve as a sample.

In *Jockie and Maggie's Courtship*, the Minister, the Kirk Session, the Kirk-treasurer, the Sackcloth, and the Cutty Stool, are all denounced in set terms. Jockie's mother anathematises the two last " as just a wheen Papish rites an' rotten ceremonies, fashing fouks wi' sacking gowns and buttock mails, an' I dinna ken what; but bide ye till I see the minister." So, too,

" Jockie, being three times summoned to the session and not appearing, the session insisted for a warrant from the justice of peace, which was readily granted, more for diversion than for justice sake. The warrant being given to John King, the constable, he went away with Clinkem Bell, on Saturday's morning, and catched John just at his brose, hauls him awa', ane at ilka oxter like twa butcher dogs hinging at a bill's beard; his mither followed, driving him up with good counsel, "my bra' man Johnny, haud up ye'r head, an' dinna think shame, for a' ye'r fauts is but perfect honesty, ye're neither a thief, nor a horse-stealer."

Poor Jockie was only a father when he should not have been one,—rather a virtue than a vice, in the eyes of his mother. Naturally enough the sin sat lightly on his conscience, and if it had not been for the 'black stool,' he would have been a happy man. On being brought before the Justice, and asked if he was willing to support the child, he cried.

"O! yes, stir, 'am no refusing to gie meat an' meal to maintain't; but my mither winna let me to the black stool," which is corroborated by the mother exclaiming:

"Ony thing ye like, stir, but that shamefu' stance, the black stool. Here's uncle Rabby, an' auld Sandy the Soutor, will be caution that we's face the Session on Sunday; the lad's wae enough that he did it, but he cannot help it now it's past, and by-hand."

The trial scene is so characteristic, that it will bear being quoted at greater length.

"On Sabbath, after sermon, the Session met. John and his mother is called upon: he enters courageously, saying, 'goode'en to you, maister minister, bellman, an' elders a'; my mither an' me is baith here.'

Mess John.—Then let her in,—come awa', goodwife. What's the reason you kept your son so long back from answering the Session? You see it is the thing you are obliged to do at last.

Mith.—Deed, stir, I think there needna be nae mair mark about it; I think when he's gien the lazy hulk, the mither o't, baith meal an' groats to maintain't, ye needna fash him; he's a dutiful father indeed, weel I wat, when he feeds his bystarts sae weel.

Mess John.—Woman, are you a hearer of the gospel, that ye reject the dictates of it? How come you to despise the discipline of the church? are not offenders to be rebuked and chastised?

Mith.—Yes, stir, a' that's very true; but I hae been three or four times through the Bible, and the New Testament, an' I never saw a repenting-stool in't a'; then whar cou'd the first of them come frae, for the Apostles had nane o' them? But a daft history book tells me that the first of them was us'd about Rome, among the Papists; an' ay when ony of them turn'd Whigs, they were put on a four-neuked thing, like a yarn-winnle blades, an' rave a' their gouls sindry till they turn'd Papists again; an then, for anger, they put them on a black stane or stool in the middle o' the Kirk, an' the seck gown about them, wi' the picture o' the de'il an' Satan on't; a sweet be wi' us, we suedna speak o' the ill thief in the Kirk! but it is a mercy the minister's here an' he come; but that was the origin o' your repenting-stools. An' when the Whigs chas'd awa' the Papist fouk out o' this kintry, they left a wheen o' their religious pictures, an' the stool of repentance was amongst the spoil; but ye's no get my bairn to set upon a thing as high as a hen-bawk, an' ilka body to be glowring at him.

Mess John.—Woman, I told you formerly, that any one who refuses submission to the government of the church is liable to excommunication."

In spite of the vigorous defence made by his mother, John is sentenced " to appear publicly on the stool of repentance on Sabbath next, and the two following thereafter, to be absolved from the scandal."

John refuses, as long as he can, to obey the sentence, but is ultimately forced to give in, when his lawful wife bears him a son, which the minister refuses to 'christen,' so long as its father remains obdurate. This lets us into the secret of much of the Kirk's authority in these cases. The superstitious faith, and transcendent efficacy, attached to the baptismal rite in the last century, were lamentably strong. In the narrative just quoted from, Marion affirms that "'tis a very uncanny thing to keep an unchristened creature about a house, or yet to meet, in the morning, a body wanting a name:" and another speaker defines the difference between "a beast and a woman's ain bairnie" to be, that "a dog is a brute beast, an' a wean is a christened creature."

Occasionally the dreaded stool was a source of amusement,—witness *John Cheap's* account of an accident that befell himself:

"On the Sabbath I went to the Kirk with the goodman, and I missed him about the door, went into the middle of the Kirk, but could see no empty seats but one big firm, where none sat but one woman by herself, and so I sat myself down beside her, not knowing where I was, until the sermon was over, when the minister began to rebuke her . . . . . ; and then she began to whinge and howl like a dog, which made me run out cursing, before the minister had given the blessing."

Towards the end of the century the power of the church to regulate morals and punish indiscretions became greatly weakened. The clergy had grown careless, dissolute and inattentive to their duties. It was no longer considered quite respectable for the better classes to take their servants along with them to church; attendance twice a day was voted a bore; and the cutty stool was ignominiously kicked out of all the 'fashionable' churches. The extracts already given indicate that the people were beginning to rebel against the tyranny of the Kirk Session, and the same spirit is even more prominent in a once popular chap-book entitled,—

"*An Account of the General Assembly's Invention for the final Extirpation of the Black-stool of Repentance and the Sackcloth Gown out of the Kirks of Scotland: purposing a new and easy* method of punishing sporting ladies. 12mo. Printed in the year 1776."

This brochure is in verse, and after a very coarse but vigorous denunciation of the stool as a thing of evil and of Popish extraction, it concludes with,—"*Maggie Beath's verdict of the original, and the dangerous tendency of the black-stool and sackcloth gown, giving an account how narrowly she escaped them, and her earnest desire to have them burnt.*"

More significant still is the whole tone of the chap-books on the subject of the 'ministers.' *Jockie and Maggie's Courtship; Janet Clinker* in her orations: old *Be-go, Sawny's* mother-in-law; *Leper,* the tailor; and *Sawny* himself: all indulge in sneers at *Mess John. Sawny* thought that "ministers might christen poor folks' bits of weans for naething, the water was no that scarce. They were well paid for their preaching, and might very well baith marry and christen a' poor fouks to the bargain, by way of mags."

§ 12. A like harshness and severity coloured the relations of private and domestic life. Parents ruled their children with a veritable rod of iron. 'Father' was a word to inspire fear and trembling, not love and affection. The head of the family was a personage of vast importance, within his own little circle. A special chair was set apart for him in the cosiest corner of the room; special dishes were served up to him at dinner, which he ate with his hat on: while his children stood respectfully uncovered in his presence and only smiled or laughed on sufferance. Hence the frequent occurrence, in early comedy and fiction, of the stern parent who insists on disposing of his son or daughter in marriage, according to his own sovereign pleasure. In the *Edinburgh Courant* for 28th October, 1758, a certain Robert McNair and his wife, Jean Holmes, advertised that, owing to the conduct of their daughter Jean in marrying without having first obtained their consent, they " thereby did discharge all and every one of their children from offering to marry without their special consent; and the child who proposed to do so would be banished for twelve months from their family; and if they did actually marry—for seven years; and in the event of a clandestine marriage, they should lose all claim of the effects, goods, gear and estate of the said Robert McNair." In the school-house, as at home, the youngsters must have had a hard time of it. Of the manner in which delinquents were flogged, a graphic account is given in the adventures of *Lothian Tom;* and there is at least one case on record of a parish dominie literally caning one of his pupils to death.

§ 13. The savage severity of the Criminal Code was rendered more oppressive to the poor, by the partial and one-sided manner in which the law was administered. In *Jockie and Maggie's Courtship,* special allusion is made to this, where the former's mother bursts into a passionate torrent of invective, on her son being adjudged to the cutty-stool; because he, being a poor man, is condemned to public shame and costs, while the young laird is allowed to indulge his amorous propensities, and, unchecked, help to people the parish with the results of his folly. But this is a mild instance of a grave disease. We read of two 'fellows' being hanged for stealing sybows or young onions,—while a forger escapes with imprisonment, because he was 'ingenuous' (*i.e.*, of good family); of a tailor in Currie being beheaded, in 1692, for marrying his *first wife's half-brother's daughter*,—while a Captain Douglas, though found guilty of a shocking assault upon a servant-maid at Glasgow in 1697, was merely fined, " he being a ' gentleman ' and engaged in the King's service." Nay! in this same year, a poor woman was actually burnt at the Old Bailey, London, for colouring a piece of metal to make it resemble a shilling.

The prisons, again, were often turned into hotels—much after the same fashion as the New York Tombs is to-day—by criminals, and debtors of the better class; and to such a length were the revelries of the jovial inmates carried, that the authorities had eventually to interfere. In 1780, one James Brown, a turnkey in the Tolbooth of Ayr, got so drunk at one of these orgies that he locked one of his prisoners outside; though half a century earlier it had been enacted by the magistrates that "prisoners within the Tolbuith be discharged from holding any feasting, treat or banquet, within the prison ; and that no person above the number of one be allowed to dine or sup with any such prisoners."

§ 14. Dr. Strang, in his *Glasgow Clubs*, gives an amusing picture of drunkenness during last century. " When dinner was over and the dessert removed—which was invariably the case after it had stood a short time—the wine bottles made a few circles, and were immediately succeeded by the largest China bowl in the house. In this gorgeous dish, which was, of course, placed before the landlord, the universal beverage of cold punch was quickly manufactured ; and towards its proper concoction many opinions were freely offered ; but to these the host, if a regular punch-maker, paid little attention. The ceremonial was gone through with great deliberation, and with an air of self-importance that must have made a stranger smile. The pleasing decoction once made, and approved of, it was now the time to sit in for serious drinking—

and serious, indeed, it often was ; for, while toast followed toast, and bowl followed bowl, it rarely happened that the party broke up till some of them, at least, were not in a condition to retire to their homes without the aid of companions who, if their heads were less muzzied, possessed more stable legs. The retiring of a guest to the drawing-room was a rare occurrence indeed; and hence the poor lady of the house was generally left to sip her tea in solitude, while her husband and friends were getting *royal* over their *sherbet. The fact is, that drinking and swearing were characteristic of the dinner parties of the last century, not only in Glasgow*, but everywhere else. To be found muzzy after dinner was too frequent, even with the most respectable; for we find that Prime Ministers were not ashamed to 'move the House' when they were tipsy; nor did some of their leading opponents blush to tell that they went to bed frequently in a state of helpless intoxication. There was a Bacchanalian stamp about the every-day life and conversation, as well as about the literature of the last century ; and the man who could talk longest about wines, and who could likewise carry off the most bottles, was looked upon with favour and admiration. It was, in fact, at that time an exception to the general rule for a man to be either willing or capable of joining the ladies after dinner." Indeed, had he wished to shirk his punch, he could hardly have done so, for the host, to prevent any one from leaving the room sober, was in the habit of locking the door and keeping the key in his pocket. The Laird of Garscadden and his friends, who thought it effeminate to rise from the table on the same day in which they sat down, were but types of the general community,—the counterpart of him whose grave-stone declares:

"Here lyes—read it with your hats on—
The bones of Bailie William Watson,
Who was famous for his thinking
And moderation in his drinking."

It was, indeed, a time of unlimited toasts and loyal bumpers; a hard-drinking, daredevil, reckless, headachy age, when, at stated periods of the evening, a boy came in to unloose the neckcloths of gentlemen who had fallen under the table; when a farmer would go into a tavern when the good wife was 'setting' a hen, and would never come out until the chickens were running about; and when there was a students' Nine-Tumbler Club in St. Andrew's University, the test of fitness for entrance into which was the ability of the candidate to articulate the words 'Bib-li-cal cri-ti-cism,' after having drunk nine tumblers of toddy. Among shop-keepers and manufacturers, even in 1800, a 'meridian' glass was an almost universal habit, while forenoon 'gilling' obtained with the humbler craftsmen. 'Gentle and simple,' tippled to excess all day; no business contract could be sealed without the stamp of the *stoup;* and worthy deacons and wealthy magistrates had their stiff tumblers of toddy before they were rightly wakened from their slumbers. A sheep could not be sold; a couple of old hats could not be 'swapped;' or the weighty matters of the Church discussed by reverend clergymen—without a tankard of two-penny, or a glass of Glenlivet. It should be borne in mind, however, that not a little of this dram-drinking resulted from the meanness of the house accommodation of the times, which drove people to taverns. Physicians or advocates, of the first position, were regularly to be seen at their respective 'houfs'; and at professional consultations, the liquor used was sherry, which was supplied in mutchkin stoups, and paid for by the client. Thus, after *Lothian Tom* had triumphed over the Edinburgh butchers in the Court of Session, he and his law-agent adjourned to a public house close by, to have a 'hearty bottle before parting.' And in *The Pleasures of Matrimony*, the mistress and her maid allow themselves to be 'treated' by a common quack, in a vulgar tavern. Ale, or whisky, or claret, was the never failing accompaniment of all the less common incidents of ordinary life. If a person were born into the world, or his soul were borne out of it; if a babe were being christened, or a rogue being hanged; by the sickbed, and in the barn; at markets and sacraments; in the churchyard, and at the altar: whisky or ale was drunk in immoderate quantities by 'gentle and simple.'

Was it a marriage? then had the bellman to be fee'd with drink; and, on leaving the church, the supporters and friends of the bride and bridegroom in *Jockie and Maggie's Courtship*, "joined thegither and cam hame in a crowd; and at every 'change-house' they chanced to pass by, Providence stopt their proceedings with full stoups, bottles and glasses, drinking their healths, wishing them much joy, ten girls and a boy. Jockie, seeing so many wishing well to his health, coupt up what he gat for to augment his health, and gar him live lang, which afterwards coupt him up, and proved detrimental to the same." The bridegroom went drunk to bed, as a matter of course; and the whole company, men and women, were in much the same condition; except poor Maggie, who, being daft, had not the sense to get intoxicated. In the *Coalman's Courtship* and *The Pleasures of Matrimony*, too, the happy man is tipsy, and in a curious tract entitled "An Accurate Description of the Marriage Ceremonies used by every Nation in the World. 12mo. Edinburgh, 1782," the newly married couple are bedded, metaphorically speaking, in a river of sack. A favourite dinner of *Sawny*, the coalman, was ale and baps; his long experience of which, however, did not prevent him from getting ingloriously drunk with old "*Be-go*, his good mother that was to be." And were not *John Cheap* and the quack Doctor so drunk for two days and two nights that they had to prick each other with pins to keep themselves awake? Then there was the night at Linlithgow, when *John* met his "sweet and dear companion, *Drouthy Tam;* and they held a most terrible encounter with the tippenny for twa nights and a day." But the vice was not confined to poor farmers and peddlers. Clergymen openly frequented the public-house in the interval between the fore and after noon services; and the annual sacramental feast was the occasion of much and wide-spread intemperance. In many places, tents for the sale of drink were erected before the kirk door; and there was a constant intercommunication between the church and dram-shop. *Janet Clinker's Orations* contains a graphic picture of the times:

Janet Clinker "aye ken'd when Sunday came round, for her father cow'd ay his beard when the bell rang, and then every body ran to the kirk that had ony thing to do, gin it were to buy saut or shune, for the chapman chiels set up a' their creims at the kirk door, and the lassies wa'd a' got keeking glasses, red snoods, needles, pins, elshin irons, gimblers, brown bread, and *black saep;* forby sweety wives' things, and rattles for restless little anes; the men wa'd a' *bought pints o' ale and gotten a whang o' gude cheese to chew i' the time o' drinking o't.* Ay, ay, there was braw markets on Sunday i' the time o' Peapery; we had nae minister then but priests, mess Johns, black friars, and white friars, monks, abbots and bishops. They had nae wives, yet the best o' them wa'd a' spoken bawdy language, and kiss'd the lassies. Fickle, sykin bodies they were, unco ill to please. They wa'd baith a' curs'd folk, and bless'd them, just as we paid them; a-deed they were unco greedy o' the penny, and prayed ay to the dead folk and gar'd the living pay them for't; and tho' they had play'd the loon wi' a puir hizzy, she durstna speak out for her very life, for they could gi'e ony body o'er to the de'il when they liket. They didna gar folk learn to read, and pray, like our new ministers, thump on your breast, strike your fingers o'er oboon your nose, tell your. beads, and rin bare-fit amang the hard stanes and cauld snaw."

This passage, in itself extremely curious and interesting, illustrates another characteristic of the times under notice, which has not yet been referred to, viz.: the Scottish intolerance and persecution of Episcopalians, Roman Catholics and Quakers. *Mrs. Clinker* must have flourished in the latter half of the seventeenth, and the beginning of the eighteenth century, for 'soap' was hardly known north of the Tweed until 1700. Her picture of the chapmen setting up their 'creims' at the kirk door, the women buying keeking glasses and snoods, and black bread, and the men drinking pints of ale and eating 'whangs o' cheese,' is vivid in the extreme. But to return to the use of drink at marriages and funerals. An Argyllshire 'burial' was often made the protest for a wild saturnalia, extending over from one to three days, and not unfrequently ending in a hand-to-hand fight between the relatives of the deceased; and it was one of these convivialities—but in high life—that resulted in the murder of Carnegie of Finhaven, in 1728.

§ 15. Intimately connected with this general excess in drinking, was the great popularity, among the better classes, of games of chance, particularly of cards and dice. The gambling mania had reached a fair height as early as 1725, about which time a company was established in Edinburgh, the partners of which made it their business to track out, and decoy young men of rank and fortune, with the view of 'plucking' them. Several years before, a well-known Jacobite won six thousand merks from Sir Alexander Gilmour, of Craigmillar, at cards, in one night; and Francis Charteris, a cadet of an ancient and honourable family in Dumfriesshire, is said to have swindled the Duchess of Queensberry out of £3,000 at one sitting, by means of a couple of mirrors placed opposite each other, in which he saw her Grace's 'hand' reflected. In 1707, Sir Andrew Ramsay, of Abbotshall, lost 28,000 merks, to Sir Scipio Hill, at cards and dice, and granted a bond upon his estate for the amount. A favourite mode in which estates were lost and won was cockfighting, a popular amusement of last century. In 1783, one Joey Payne kept a celebrated cock-pit at Rutherglen Loan, near Glasgow; and among the keenest enthusiasts in the brutal sport was the then Duke of

Hamilton and Brandon. The game was introduced into Scotland about 1702, at which time a cock-pit was in operation in Leith Links; the charges of admission to which were 10d. for the front row, 7d. for the second, and 4d. for the third. Soon after, according to Arnot, the historian of Edinburgh, the passion for cock-fighting became so general among all ranks of the people, that the magistrates of that city 'discharged' its being practised in the streets, on account of the disturbances it occasioned. So late as 1800, the boys attending the parish schools were in the habit of bringing cocks to school at Fasten's E'en (Shrovetide), when the whole day was devoted to the sport, in presence of the minister of the parish and his reverend friends. So universal was this custom, that the cock-fight dues formed, in some instances, one of the most valuable sources of the dominie's income, being equal to one quarter's payment for each scholar. But the great and most general outlet for the joyous feelings of the community, was afforded by the 'fairs,' or markets, which were held once or twice a year, with great spirit and bustle, in every parish in Scotland. Many of these are still kept up in country districts, but they have lost their old importance and character. In earlier times the 'fair' was looked forward to by the whole country side with anxiety and hope; and preparations for it were made months beforehand. To them resorted packmen from all parts, bearing with them the fine stuffs of Flanders; feminine apparel from England; shawls from Paisley; and wares of all kinds from many lands. To them, too, came the goodwife to lay in her annual stock of clothes and household goods; the farmer to sell or purchase cattle and agricultural implements; the maiden to buy herself new finery, and get a husband, or a new 'place,'—in any case a 'fairing' from some admiring swain; with a miscellaneous crowd, to be counted by thousands, whose main object was what the Irish call 'divarshun.' One of the best known and most characteristic of these gatherings was the great Ayrshire fair of Kirkdamdie, celebrated in history and song, which was held from time immemorial on the green knoll beside the ruins of the chapel in Kirkdamdie, on the last Saturday of May. The day before the fair was one of great preparation and bustle. Innumerable booths and stands for the sale of refreshments and merchandise were in course of erection all over the place; from earliest dawn, scores of packmen on foot, and their more honoured rivals on horse, were arriving with their bales of merchandise from every airt, and wrangling with the rapacious harpies who levied the market duties of them; while, from the various pathways across the hills, or down the straths, the plaided and bonneted population kept pouring in all the day on foot, on horseback, and in rude carts,— the maidens gay in their 'Sunday braws,' and having their waists clasped by swarthy swains; and every face wearing a look of anxiety and joy. So late as 1800, the number of tents at Kirkdamdie was from forty to fifty, and the fair was one of considerable interest and size even in 1847, since which time its glories have paled before the rising importance of its rival at Girvan. This, in short, was the Donnybrook of Scotland; and the license which was allowed at these saturnalia gave rise to no little immorality and vice, as well as to innumerable pitched battles in which from fifty to a hundred combatants took part on each side, with sticks and stones.

Previous to the Reformation, the popular amusements consisted chiefly of 'Robin Hood and Little John' Games, the 'Abbot of Unreason,' 'Ye runeboles and tuilzeing the same,' 'Lady Templeton,' music, dancing, athletic sports, wappinshaws, masquerades, dramatic performances, with recitations of ballads, and telling of tales. When golf, shinty and football came into vogue is not definitely known, but references to them occur at a very early period, and horse-racing was introduced into Ayrshire as early as 1698. In the flood of the Reformation, these amusements were all but utterly swept away, and a heavy gloom fell upon the land. The lute and the guitar were heard no more beneath fair ladies' casements by moonlight; the bagpipe sobbed and wailed amid remote recesses, into which the fury of the reformers had driven it; and the heel-inspiring fiddle was laid upon the shelf to wait the return of happier times. No more did hooded shepherds blow their buckhorns and their cornpipes, what time they led their fat flocks out to the green pastures; or make the bosky dell and daisied hollow resound with their sweet strains in praise of Amaryllis. Where be the goodly songs, the right merry conceits, the pleasant tales and jests, in which our rural ancestors, before John Knox, delighted? *The Tale of the Well of the World's End*, of the noble *Earl of Flanders who Wedded the Devil*, of the *Red Giant with Three Heads*, of the *Three-Footed Dog of Norway*, and the *Bold Braband*, and *The Three Weird Sisters*, and *The Four Sons of Aymon?* Gone, with their wild richness of romantic fable, their Gothic magnificence and superstition, their childish wonders,—and not a line left to give us a hint of their marvellous treasures. Then was the golden age of rustic felicity and song, when the shepherds told their pleasant stories all, and, with their wives, sang sweet melodious songs of natural music of the antiquite,—excelling in rhythmic beauty even those bewitching strains that erst were warbled by the four mermaidens when Thetis married on Mount Pelion. Nay, Orpheus himself did never pipe more dulcet notes than sang these simple shepherds and their wives what time the world was young. So runs the narrative in the *Complaynt of Scotland,* in the list of lost lyrics given in which are several, the very sound of which is redolent of the freshness of the golden prime. Such are those beginning:—"Still under the leavés green," "Broom, broom on hill," and "Cou thou me the rashes green." But with all their rustic beauty and animation, these early songs were, as a rule, gross and sensual, and stood in as much need of reform as did the Church itself. At first, indeed, the Muse was one of the most potent agents in reducing the Romish Church to ruins, by satirising the licentiousness of her ministers, and the folly of her rites. But, in course of time, she grew more indolent, and when there were left no monks or friars to attack, she turned her arrows upon the reformers themselves, and ridiculed their puritanic grimness and austerity. The latter retaliated, and preached a crusade against ungodly songs,—turning the devil's weapons against himself, by composing sacred words to profane airs, like "The Bonny Broom," "Maggie Lauder," "I'll Never Leave Thee," and "We'll go pu' the Heather." Having interfered with the Muse, it was not to be expected that the Kirk would leave the Stage alone. At first, its interference went no farther than to prevent the acting of plays upon Sunday, and to direct the drama into profane, instead of scriptural, channels. This was in 1574, but not many years elapsed before the production of stage plays and mysteries was altogether prohibited; and persons who assisted at their presentation were liable to be excommunicated, and otherwise punished. This continued till well on in the seventeenth century, when symptoms of a revival of interest in the dramatic literature began to manifest themselves. Men must laugh sooner or later, and the asceticism and self-denial of the Reformation were slowly but surely modified and mellowed by returning sweetness and light. In 1715, a company of players performed nightly at the Tennis Court, near Holyrood Palace, to 'the great grief of all sober good people;' and especially of certain pious clergymen, who excited considerable commotion by their resolution to refuse the usual sacramental tokens to such of their congregation as were known to attend these plays. The Tennis Court Company did not hold their ground long, and no theatricals of any importance were presented again till 1725, when Anthony Aston established a theatre in the same city, Edinburgh, for the production of light comedy. In 1728, Aston's troupe visited Glasgow, where they performed the *Beggars' Opera*, but received so little support that the receipts did not suffice to pay the music. For many years afterwards the drama made very slow progress in the West. In 1780, a theatre was erected outside the burgh of Glasgow, which was to be opened by the celebrated Mrs. Bellamy, and great preparations were made for that event. Unfortunately, on the night preceding that fixed for the inaugural ceremony, the house was fired by some rabid incendiaries, and the whole interior, scenery and dresses, including Mrs. Bellamy's wardrobe, valued at £900, were completely destroyed. The conflagration was the result of the intemperate oratory of a field preacher, who roused the passions of the public, by narrating a vision, which he professed to have had, of an infernal banquet, at which he heard Satan propose "the health of Mr. Miller of Westerton, who had so nobly sold his ground to build thereon a Temple of Belial, and which was to be opened for worship the very next day, so that they might thereafter reign there in triumph." And this after twenty-eight years' experience of the drama! For in 1752 a wooden theatre had been erected, persons going to and returning from which had to be guarded by detachments of constabulary, to protect them from maltreatment by the rabble. Early in the century, dancing assemblies were instituted in Edinburgh and Glasgow, and continued to flourish for many years. About 1779 the glory of the Glasgow assembly began to wane, and on March 25th of that year the following notice appeared in the *Glasgow Mercury:*

"NOTICE.—THE GLASGOW ASSEMBLY.

"The Assemblies of late have been so little frequented, that it begins to be doubted whether that kind of diversion is agreeable to the public, or whether the *gentlemen,* by too intense an application to their glass, may not have impaired their *loco-motive Faculties.* There is, however, to be a DANCING ASSEMBLY upon Thursday, the *first of April.* If it be well attended they will be continued as formerly."

The date 'first of April' throws some suspicion on the good faith of this notice, but in any case it is suggestively characteristic of the times. Music and dancing have, from time immemorial, been the favorite exercise of the Scottish people. Even stern old Cameronians, who regarded the rural dances in barns with something akin to horror, were often content to wink at the attendance of their sons on these festive gatherings. But song and dance, and the rhythmic invocation with which the fisher dropped his net into the deep, or the maiden moved her sickle through the corn, all went down before the fierce tide of the Reformation, which swept the land clear of laughter and song, of May-day sports and Christmas spectacles, and other harmless festivities and games. Almost the sole means of relaxation left to the common people was the recitation of tales and ballads, by semi-professional peasants, who took the place of the old minstrels; and, of course, a generous indulgence in the ale stoup.

§ 16. What has been said is sufficient to indicate roughly the general condition of the country. from, say 1720 to 1770. What it was at the earlier of these dates is pithily described by a writer in the *Edinburgh Review*, of July, 1867: "The nobility, far too numerous for the country, were poor place-hunters; the gentry wandering adventurers. There was no agriculture worthy of the name; no trade save what was carried on by petty peddlers. Prices were high; severe scarcities frequent. Slavery, though in theory illegal, was really enforced. All colliers and salt-makers were regarded as predial serfs. Kidnapping was a regular trade. Donacha Dhu, in the *Heart of Midlothian*, is no exaggeration. There were almost no magistrates; roads only between the large cities; rarely bridges; a greater number of idiots than in any other country; and, finally, in all times a tenth, in evil days a fifth, of the whole population, begging from door to door, living in the constant commission of every kind of crime,— a state of things so appalling that (as is well known) a regular system of slavery seemed to Fletcher, of Saltoun, the only efficient remedy for miseries so deeply rooted." This, of course, is meant to apply to the close of the seventeenth century, but it holds true, with almost equal force, of a much later period. Broadly speaking, the Scotch were an austere, church-going, minister-fearing, ale-drinking, brave, honest, coarse-mannered, muscular, and indelicate people; full of a sturdy independence of character; an unswerving love of liberty; and a deep craving for larger life and light and sunshine, which was beginning to burst the shackles, so long imposed upon them by the Puritanic enactments and prejudices of the age. Hand-in-hand with great parade and a vulgar display of dress, went vulgarity of speech and act, and under a pharisaical observance of certain religious rites were hidden immorality, profanity, and drunkenness. Ladies went to church in full dress, and got flushed and talkative after dinner, and the most outspoken language was used regarding marriages and births. Adults had few intelligent books to read, and youths were taught chiefly the catechism and psalms. Much of the indelicacy in the upper, and immorality in the lower ranks of society, resulted from the smallness of the house accommodation. Even in the last decade of the century, wealthy Glasgow merchants lived in houses which had only one public room, one or two bedrooms, and a kitchen. The family had their meals in one of the bedchambers, and the public apartment was only used when company were being entertained. Dinner was served at from one to three o'clock, P. M., and at six the hostess entertained her gossips to tea, while her husband went off to his club in the tavern, where he sat drinking, and discussing the questions of the day, till nine, the hour at which these meetings usually broke up. In the country, few houses contained more than one room, supplemented in some instances by a loft and barn. The floor was of earth; the fire of peat, in the centre of the room; a hole in the roof the chimney; and along one side of the wall were two rude beds, the remaining couches being on the floor. Families slept 'heads and thraws,' and Chaucer's tale of the miller and the two clerks was too frequently enacted in real life. The coarseness of the conversation between persons of opposite sexes surpasses belief, and the dialogue in *Jockie and Maggie's Courtship*, and *The Coalman's Courtship*, is only a literal, short-hand report of what might be heard any day in almost any clachan in the land. In *John Cheap the Chapman*, John bargains with the servant-girl in a house which he visits, for the use of her bed; and on being turned out of it by three drovers, lies down by the fire, while the girl sleeps with her master and mistress. In *Leper the Tailor*, in addition to a large household of men and women who sleep in the same room, an adventurous calf finds temporary shelter. The old women and widows had but one object in life, to get married, and their instructions to their children, regarding the mysteries of marriage, are as plain and outspoken as language can make them. The want of amusements, with which to wile away the long nights; the habit of whole households living together in one room; the loose morality of the age; the general and intemperate use of ale; the license allowed at country gatherings, penny weddings, and fairs; and such indecent customs as that of 'bedding' young couples, and 'touzzling' among the hay: combined to produce an amount of immorality and illegitimacy which cannot be too much deplored. Worse still, the dread of the cutty-stool drove many mothers to murder their offspring, or to contract irregular marriages, to which the free-and-easy laws on the subject held out many and powerful inducements. On *Jockie* asking his mother if he should confess to being the father of the bairn, the old hag replies:

" Ay, ay, confess ye did it, but say but ance, *an'*

that it was on the terms o' marriage, the way that a' our kintry bystarts is gotten."

Marriage might be celebrated in many ways. In the *Coalman's Courtship*, the mother says:

"But Sawny man, what way is thou gaun to do, will ye mak' a pay penny wedding, or twa three guid nibours, a peck o' meal baken with a cheese, and a barrel o' ale,—will that do?

"*Sawny.*—Na, na, mither. I'll tak' a cheaper gate nor ony o' them; I'll gar half-a-crown and a half mutchkin, or a rake o' coals do it a' [. . .]."

The manner in which Sawny did get married was as follows:

"It was agreed, over a dinner of dead fish, that the wedding was to be upon Wednesday—no bridal fouks but the twa mithers and themselves twa. So, according to appointment, they met at Edinburgh, where Sawny got the Cheap Priest, who gave them twa-three words, and twa-three lines, took their penny and a good drink, wished them joy, and gaed his wa's. 'Now,' said auld Be-go, 'if that be your minister, he's but a drunken ——, mony a ane drinks up a', *but he leaves naething;* he's got that penny for devil a haet; *ye might hae cracket lufes on't,* tane ane anither's word, a kiss and a hoddle at a hillock side, and been as well, if no better. I hae seen some honest men say mair o'er their brose nor what he said a' thegither, but an' ye be pleased, 'am pleased; a bout in the bed ends a', and maks firm work, sae here's to you and joy to the bargain,—it's ended now, weel I wat.'"

Jockie and *Maggie*, being in a better social position than *Sawny* and his bride, get married in legal and regular form: the precentor being fee'd, the bellman treated to a 'gill,' and the bans put up in the Kirk three times.

The ordinary food of the common people was coarse and scanty: Brose in the morning; brose, or ale and baps, or herring, for dinner; and brose or sowens, at night. Even in the upper classes any unusual attention to cookery was thought to be inconsistent with the spiritual destinies of man, and food was cooked in a rude and careless fashion.

§ 17. So far, only the dark side of the picture has been presented. But there are many rays of light and sunshine to relieve its dismal and sombre colours. Much of the coarseness already dwelt upon was the coarseness of health, rude and undisciplined, and possessed by the Scotch in common with other civilized nations of the time. Beneath the austere and formal harshness of the age beat warm and passionate hearts; yearning unconsciously after more warmth and light; full of a sublime love of personal, civil, and, in a mistaken way, religious liberty; and animated, on the whole, by a deep reverence for the holiest of all books, and an implicit faith in the omnipotence, though too little, perhaps, in the mercy of a divine Providence. Their vulgarity was the result of imperfect education; their indecency and drunkenness, the inevitable revulsion from the too severe and bitter tyranny of Kirk and State. Torn by civil and religious strifes; forced to win their bread with their right hand ever on their sword-hilt; oppressed and hungered by famines and sieges and the unrighteousness of men in office; engaged in an intermittent hand-to-hand and foot-to-foot struggle with the ever clamorous armies of kingcraft, priestcraft, popery, and the devil—is it to be wondered at that, when after the Union, the country began to emerge from this ocean of bloodshed and famine and peril, its inhabitants were ignorant and rude, behind in arts and commerce, and not so well educated in the *bienséances* of society as were their rivals across the Tweed? Rather let us admire the splendid patience, the indomitable perseverance, the sublime obstinacy in the cause of liberty, the sterling independence of character, and honesty of purpose, that enabled this people, so scattered and poor in numbers and resources, to preserve their spirit unbroken through crises so tremendous; and, after a fierce and long-protracted struggle with more powerful foes, to achieve and maintain religious liberty, and complete political independence. From the day on which the Union was completed and ratified, date the commercial greatness and social prosperity of Scotland. On that day was consummated, at least potentially, the work the Revolution had begun—the comparative annihilation of the power of the nobles. As the aristocracy were depressed and circumscribed, the people acquired liberty, and rose to something like dignity and power. With the establishment of the parochial system of schools, education spread through the masses; with peace, and freedom from civil and religious broils, commerce grew from more to more, until its ships made white far distant seas; and the healthy rivalry which sprang up between the two countries powerfully stimulated the trade of both. Glasgow rose, almost at a bound, to be the great manufacturing metropolis of Scotland, and to all but monopolise the tobacco trade with America. In 1709 and 1711, respectively, appeared the first numbers of the *Tatler* and *Spectator;* in 1731, the *Gentleman's Magazine;* and 1749, the first English Review, the *Monthly.* Allan Ramsay, in 1735, founded the first regular circulating library in Britain; in 1699, the first Scottish newspaper that showed vitality was started under the title of the *Edinburgh Gazette*, followed in 1705, by the *Edinburgh Courant.* About the same time the banking system was greatly developed, and in 1711 the post office was extended to Scotland. The good effects of these measures were slow to show themselves. Many years elapsed before their influences were made publicly manifest; and from 1715 to 1745, English jealousy excluded the Scotch from participating in the colonial trade,

Scotland being treated more as a conquered province, than an independent country on an equal footing with its wealthier rival. But, though the good seed was long of coming to maturity, its progress was almost miraculously rapid when it did begin to ripen, and the harvest proved to be one of astonishing fertility and wealth.

> "I, wha stand here in this bare, shabby coat,
> Was once a packman, worth mony a groat;
> I've carried packs as big as your ha' table,
> I've scrapit pats and sleepit in a stable;
> Six pounds I wadna for my pack ance ta'en,
> And I would boldly brag it was a' my ain.
> Aye, thae were days indeed that gar'd me hope
> Aiblins, through time, to warsell up a shop."
> —*The Loss o' the Pack.*

CHAPTER II.

§ 1. *Early literature of Scotland.—Minstrelsy in the olden time.*
§ 2. *Minstrelsy and the Reformation. — Origin of the literary chap-man.*
§ 3. *Origin of the humorous chap-book.—Scottish literature from Ramsay to Burns.*
§ 4. *Character of the chap-books.—Chap-books historically valuable.—Stationery stores in the Salt-market in the eighteenth century.*
§ 5. *The Chapman.—Qualifications of a successful chap-man.—Peter Duthie.*
§ 6. *Classification. — Humorous chap-books.*
§ 7. *Instructive chap-books.*
§ 8. *Romantic chap-books.*
§ 9. *Superstitious chap-books.*
§ 10. *Authorship of chap-books.*

§ 1. Few literatures are so rich in story and song as that of Scotland. From the earliest times, of which any record exists, there was a large stock of unrecorded fiction and song floating about among all classes, the great bulk of which has, unfortunately, perished. Barbarous, or half-civilized communities, delight, like children, to revel in marvels of adventure and romance. The list of tales and songs given in the *Complaynt of Scotland*, as having been in existence in the middle of the sixteenth century, is a sufficient index to the kind of literature most popular with the people of those days. Chaucer, Ovid, and the Arthurian legends furnished no small portion of the stock; while Mandeville, Virgil, and Æsop contributed their respective quota. Among the stories most common were: 'Robert le Diable', 'Ferrand, Earl of Flanders, that married the Devil,' 'The Red Etin with the Three Heads,' 'The Well of the World's End,' 'The Three-footed Dog of Norroway,' 'Tale of How the King of Eastmoreland married the King's Daughter of Westmoreland,' 'The Four Sons of Aymon,' 'The Brig of the Manbrybill,' 'Sir Walter, the bold Lesley,' 'Bevis of Southampton,' 'Young Tamlane and the bold Braband,' 'Sir Egeir and Sir Gryme,' 'Tale of the Three Weird Sisters,' 'The Golden Apple,' 'Hero and Leander,' 'Pyramus and Thisbe,' 'The Sieges of Tyre, Thebes, Troy, and Milan,' 'Wallace,' 'Bruce,' 'Ipomydon,' 'The Prophecies of Merlin, the Rhymer, Bede and Marlyng,' and 'Robin Hood and Little John.' There were also versions of the nursery tales of 'Jack the Giant Killer,' and 'Cinderella,' entitled respectively 'The Giants that Eat Quick Men' and 'The Tale of the Pure Tint;' the latter of which furnished the groundwork of the 'Pure Tint of Rashy-coat,' printed by the late Robert Chambers in his *Popular Rhymes of Scotland*. In addition to these, and similar narratives, there existed a large number of songs and several astrological almanacks. The above tales were mostly in verse, that being the form most easily remembered, and were circulated among the people orally, by professional bards or minstrels, who gained a livelihood from their recitation. Of such was blind Harry, who, with Hog, Watschod, and Wedderspune, was attached to the Court of James IV. as tale-teller. These errant-minstrels combined the characters of musician and bard, and, harp in hand, wandered from castle to castle, and hamlet to hamlet, reciting to lord and peasant, gentle and simple, their legends of love and war. Welcome guests were they in cottage and hall; beloved by the people, and regarded as a privileged class. In the *Scotichronicon*, written about 1441, Bower laments that the vulgar crowd of his own day took great delight in plays, ballads, and romances, founded on the story of *Robin Hood and Little John;* and there is authentic evidence that 'gests' were written upon important political and social events, and on the adventures and lives of men like Bruce and Wallace. But the majority of these productions have perished, for the clergy, to whom was entrusted the exclusive preservation of literature in writing, were the sworn foes of the minstrels, whom they looked upon as impudent varlets, and servants of the prince of darkness. Even after the introduction of printing in the sixteenth century, a long time elapsed before any serious attempt was made to preserve the popular tales and ballads. The early typographers were deeply impressed with the importance of their art, and cared not to put it to what, in their fresh enthusiasm, they might easily have deemed to be ignoble uses. A world of classical learning and poetry called imperatively for their first attention; the wisdom and wit of Greece, Rome, Palestine, and Chaucer, were waiting impatiently to be printed in the Scottish tongue; and the slighter forms had even to wait their turn. Hence it is that the works described in the *Complaynt of Scotland* have, in most cases, perished; and of the songs and ballads only a few scattered lines remain to tantalise us with their poetic suggestiveness.

§ 2. For some time previous to the Reformation minstrelsy had begun to fall into comparative disrepute, and about 1550 severe measures were passed, which interfered greatly with the excercise of the craft, and all but suppressed the sports of the commonalty. Nine years later, the long pent-up fires burst their thin crust, and flamed forth into the fierce volcano of Reform, in whose scorching heat the poor old tales of superstition and romance, the songs and ballads of the people which had gladdened Scottish hearts for twice two hundred years, were shrivelled up, and perished. When, however, the rigour of the reformation began to abate, the minds of the people turned instinctively to their old amusements. The minstrels, of course, were gone, but by and by their places began to be supplied by semi-professional reciters or singers, who supplemented their ordinary labours in the field and on the hill, by visiting the various farm houses in their neighborhood, to delight the rustic inmates with their rude stories and jests. Ultimately, when the wants of the people increased, and printing was applied to the multiplication of broadsides and black-letter tracts, the itinerant peddlers, who were then almost the only merchants in the country, began to unite the functions of salesmen and story-tellers, and by their means, the cheap tracts, histories, songs, and collections of facetiæ, which then constituted the sole literary pabulum of the multitude, were circulated throughout the country. Towards the middle and end of the last century, this sort of trade reached its highest point of prosperity, and flying stationers were welcome guests in every house and hamlet. The circumstances of the country, and the state of the roads between the towns and remote districts, rendered the packmen absolutely necessary; and experience taught them to be accommodating and polite to their different customers. No business depended more for success upon courteous manners than did the travelling merchant's; there was a 'knack' necessary, neither to be too pressing nor too careless about selling, never to look disappointed nor annoyed if unable to obtain purchasers, and never to fail in good humour, however tried and harassed.

About this time, too, an immense stimulus was given to the circulation of this vulgar literature by the extraordinary vigour and humour of a humble peddler, who took to writing, editing, and publishing chap-books.

§ 3. This man was Dougal Graham, sometime bellman to the city of Glasgow, better known as the author of a metrical history of the Rebellion of 1745-6, and who flourished from about 1724 to 1779. Until Graham's advent, chap-books had consisted chiefly of almanacks, songs, theological and political tracts, and nursery tales, with collections of facetiæ and romantic legends, common to all European and many Asiatic countries. But Graham introduced what may almost be called a revolution in this sort of literature. His long experience of the lower classes, in his capacity of peddler, and his intimate knowledge of their likings, prejudices, and customs, combined with a natural itch for writing, and considerable humour and descriptive power, first inspired him with the idea of turning his experiences to account and catering to the vulgar taste. With this end, he collected many of the stories then current, and worked them up into a connected form, giving them a local colouring, and a coarse flavour, that suited them to the tastes of his humble patrons. In other cases, he seized on some of the most common customs of the poor, and wove around them a humorous thread of narrative; or, following the example of Chaucer, Shakespeare, and Milton, boldly stole an original, and, if possible, foreign work,— clothed it anew in Scottish dress, and gave it to the world as his own. In the absence of the date of imprint on most of the early chap-books, it is seldom possible to say which were the first editions; but the *conscensus* of opinion on the subject assigns the majority of the most humorous and characteristic chap-books to the period which elapsed from the death of Allan Ramsay, towards the middle of the century, to the time when the poems of Burns began to obtain a firm footing in the country. This interval, stretching over more than fifty years, was all but barren in literary effort, and the absence of anything in the shape of cheap literature, except a few fugitive tracts and songs, if it did not altogether originate, gave, at any rate, an immense impulse to the production and circulation of chap-books. Towards the end of the seventeenth, and the beginning of the eighteenth century, the libraries of poor folk consisted of only a Bible, the Confession of Faith, a bunch of ballads, and *Sir William Wallace*,—the first for the gudewife, the second for the gudeman, the third for the daughter, and the last for the son. Metrical versions of *Robin Hood*, Barbour's *Bruce*, and individual ballads, with now and then a small collection of songs, formed the staple literary—almost, indeed, the only popular entertainment, especially in rural districts. As education spread and civilization advanced, the number of readers steadily and rapidly increased, and the old supply of literary pabulum was found to be insufficient. This want was the more felt owing to the dominance of priestcraft, and the austerity with which all sports and amusements were regarded, causing young and old, particularly in the country, to crave for some other means of enjoyment and mirthful relaxation than was afforded by the recitation of ballads, the bandying about of rude jokes, and the coarse customs which obtained in connection with certain seasons of the year. Deprived of a legitimate outlet for their social activities, and having much spare time on their hand, the youth of both sexes were driven to seek excitement in a rude, broad style of talk and intercourse, which led to many serious evils. Still more was the want of cheap, amusing books felt when the death of the 'gentle shepherd,' who had so long delighted Scotland with his artless pipings on the oaten reed, left the people without any prominent popular literary purveyor. Then it was that, naturally and without any special movement or guidance, the humorous chap-literature of

Scotland sprang into sudden and vigorous vitality, bridging over the gulf which separates the Ballad from the daily and periodical Press. From London, Newcastle, Stirling, Edinburgh, Glasgow, Paisley, Irvine, and Kilmarnock, the country was inundated with a continuous and constantly increasing flood of chap-books, the annual issue of which, in Scotland alone, is supposed by Mr. Chambers to have exceeded 200,000; a calculation greatly within the mark. They had a place by every fireside; their incidents and jokes were on every tongue; in farm-house and hamlet they formed the chief amusement of thousands; and in spite of their grossness and profanity, their ridicule of 'Mess John,' and their contempt of superiors, no attempt was made by the ecclesiastical or civil authorities to interfere with their production or circulation. This continued till early in the present century, when the introduction of cheap and wholesome literature effected naturally, quietly, and efficiently, a reform which, although never before advocated, was greatly needed, and drove the coarser chap-books across the border, where they found a refuge in Newcastle and the North of England. By this, it is not meant that these publications were abolished. They are still circulated in large numbers throughout the country, but the more indecent have been weeded out, and almost all of them have been expurgated and revised, while their sale is becoming yearly more circumscribed and limited.

§ 4. The early chap-books should be read in the light of the age which gave them birth. Coarse in nature and gross in language and morals, people told stories in the family circle, and without any thought of offence, which might have caused Boccaccio or him of the Golden Ass to blush. Of this coarseness we have a graphic—at times, too graphic reflex—in the class of books under review, some of which, and these the most characteristic and popular, are so broad, one can only wonder that the austere *custodes morum* of the times ever allowed them to be openly circulated and read, without an effort to check, or abate the evil. The best apology that can be made for this coarseness is, that the indecencies were unconscious—the freedoms and liberties of a child rolling on a carpet. These works meant no evil, and took no thought of the laughter of remote critics; being addressed to a rude, healthy, half-educated audience, in want of amusement and craving to have their midriffs tickled. In this they succeeded, and their historical value is partly due to this occasional disregard of what are now regarded as the proprieties. In a curious sketch of a 'Bookseller's Establishment of the Olden Time,' which occurs in a book entitled *Aberdeen Worthies*, written by William Bannerman, and published before 1840, a brief list is given of books most popular towards the end of last century, and sold in "the little shopie aside the Plainstanes," in Aberdeen. One part of the sole window in the establishment was occupied with favourite schoolboy authors, and such coarse but attractive prints of the day as 'The Farm Yard on Fire,' 'The Mad Bull,' 'Haymaking,' 'Harvest Home,' and the like, "price twopence coloured or one penny plain; printed and sold by Carrington & Bowles, 45 St. Paul's Churchyard." These prints were to be found all over Europe, and at the present moment the children of the members of that firm are in receipt of a handsome independence derived from the sale of these little publications. Side by side with the above were such stock pieces as 'The History of King Pippin,' and 'The Death of Cock Robin,' with cuts, and bound in gilt, price one penny; and above them, again, the larger volumes, including, in prose, 'The History of Lothian Tom,' 'Wise Willie and Witty Eppie,' 'The Sayings and Doings, and Witty Jests of George Buchanan,' 'Sir William Wallace,' etc.; in verse, 'Chevy Chase,' 'The Cherry and the Slae,' 'Sir James the Rose,' 'The Dominie Deposed,' and 'Ajax's Speech to the Grecian Knabs.' The lad, who is supposed to enter the shop, asks for 'Lothian Tom,' from which it may reasonably be inferred that *Tom* was one of the most popular 'chaps' then known. About the year 1780, according to *Senex* in his 'Glasgow, Past and Present,' the old Saltmarket street bibliopolists confined themselves mostly to religious works, and to the interesting pamphlets and histories of 'Jack the Giant Killer,' 'Valentine and Orson,' 'Leper the Tailor,' 'The Seven Wise Men of Gotham,' and such like. Their premises were situated in the dark recesses under the pillars, and their establishments were decked out with assortments of half-penny prints, and gold-feuilled children's books, such as ' Goody two Shoes,' ' Babes in the Wood,' ' Puss in Boots,' ' Robinson Crusoe,' etc. The most striking article of their display, however, was the celebrated painted penny print of *Paul Jones* shooting a sailor, who attempted to strike his colours; and the miserable countenance of poor *Jack* when the pistol was being presented to his head, never failed to attract a fair assemblage of window gazers.

§ 5. In a volume of Scottish sketches entitled " Round the Grange Farm ; or, Good Old Times," by Miss Jean L. Wilson, and published by William P. Nimmo, Edinburgh, 1872, we are introduced to a very dramatic and truthfully painted picture of the conventional chapman, which may well stand as a companion sketch to that of the great prince of peddlers, whom the reader will find depicted at full length in Chapter III. Old *Dauvit* was a middle-sized, broad-shouldered man, with a keen, pawky eye, and a very sleek, worldly face. He was always clad in a blue coat like a large surtout, with big metal buttons, homespun grey vest and trousers, while his head was surmounted by a huge broad bonnet with a red top; round his neck he wore a green and yellow Indian neckerchief, which encircled his unbleached shirt collar. The lappels of his coat and vest pockets were the only fanciful part of his dress; his pack was tied in a linen table-cover, and slung over his shoulders, but *Dauvit* strode on as if he felt no burden, planting his staff firmly on the ground, and keeping a sharp eye on business. His stock consisted, perhaps, of hardware goods, comprising *five bawbee* knives, needles, pins of all sizes, from the small 'minikin' to the large ' Willie Cossar;' thimbles, scissors, bone combs, specks; also ballads, such as 'Gill Morice' and 'Sir James the Rose,' or four and eight page pamphlets, generally comprehending among the number 'John Cheap the Chapman,' 'The King and the Cobbler,' and 'Ali-Baba, or the Forty Thieves.' *Dauvit* had his regular 'rounds,' which he traversed twice, or it might be many times a year; usually contriving at nightfall to reach some friendly farmhouse, where the cog of porridge and bed of straw were cheerfully given in return for his budget of news, his packet of chap-books, or small parcel of tea and sugar, bespoken on his last visit. Every person, from the peer to the peasant, welcomed and encouraged *Dauvit* to castle or cot. When he entered a house he had always a suitable remark to set off his rustic bow, and confident familiar smile. 'Uncommon fine weather, mistress,' was his favourite salutation, varying the 'fine' with 'coarse,' 'cauld,' 'dry,' 'wat,' or 'changeable,' to suit the weather. Then followed some complimentary remark, such as—" I needna ask if ye're weel the day, for ye're the very picture o' health;" or some decidedly pleasant observation, especially to the young lasses, as, "fair fa' your bonny face, I haena seen your match in a' the borders;" or, "Eh, now! but a sight of you's a gude thing; I wonder if I ha'e ony nice ribbon in my pack for you the day," with, it might be, " Ye're a comely lassie. I wish he saw you, the noo, that likes ye best." Of course, after such flattering speeches *Dauvit* was asked to lay down his pack and give them his news, and then he, nothing loath, opened up his budget of information, told the mistress when he last saw her married daughter, and how she was looking; delivered the message to Jenny the kitchenmaid, received from some far away brother; or told the master all about the various 'craps' upon the different farms he passed through, generally ending with—" I ha'e seen nae pasture to compare wi' your ain," or, " Ye've braw corn, maister, in the park down there." He was generally asked to join the family of the small farmer at meals; but he was a very moderate eater and well bred in his own fashion, handing all the plates of bread to the company at table till told again and again "that he was eatin' nane his sel' but only watchin' other folk." *Dauvit* learned about all the marriages likely to take place, and throwing himself in the way of the bridegroom or bride, would make him or her a present of a ribbon or neckerchief; then, after a joke and an encomium on the absent one, expressing his certainty that two such "weel doin' industrious young folk couldna but be happy," he would inform them that he "was aye at hame frae the last Monday o' the a'e month to the first Monday o' the other; or, if they wad either write what they wanted, or come owre, he wad gi'e them some grand bargains," adding "that he wad tak' the siller as they could gi'e him it." .But Geordie Johnston o' the Shaw remarked, after doing, as he termed it, a "gude stroke wi' *Dauvit*," that "he wasna sae accommodatin' as he made believe." When business was over, if he could reach another farm-town before dark, he would roll up the pack, and wishing them all 'a gude afternoon,' speed on his way; but if it was near nightfall, he remained and spent the evening, sitting with the assembled household round the fire, retailing his news, or it might be slyly, but faithfully, delivering a message or letter to some lad or lass, amongst the company, from an absent sweetheart. The *fore supper* was the best time for gossip, and this, during winter, was from *lowsin'* time, about five o'clock, until eight, when the cows were milked and the horses *suppered*. All eagerly listened to *Dauvit's* summary of news, as well they might, for his budget was varied, extending from Parliamentary discussion to domestic cookery; the *bairns* listening so intently and so quietly, that they generally fell asleep on their stools, while the older part of the audience, unwilling to break the thread of his narrative, scarcely interrupted him with a single question.

No one who is at all familiar with Scottish character can fail to appreciate the truth and vigour of this sketch; which, however, gives less prominence to what may be called the artistic and literary qualifications of the peddler, than is quite suited to our immediate purpose. A better representative of the literary chap-man is to be found in a twenty-four-paged tract, entitled " Memoirs of the late John Kippen, Cooper, in Methven, near Perth, to which is added An Elegy on Peter Duthie, who was upwards of eighty years a Flying Stationer: Stirling, Printed by C. Randall,"—in which we have a curious list of the qualifications and most popular wares of the flying stationer. Peter Duthie, the subject of the elegy, flourished from 1721 till 1812, and the lines refer to the precise period under notice :

> Lament ye people, ane an' a',
> For Peter Duthie's e'en awa';
> Nae mair will Pate e'er travel round
> The circle o' his native ground;
> Nae mair shall he last speeches cry,
> Nor in the barns will ever lie;
> Nae mair shall he again appear
> To usher in the infant year,
> With *Almanacks* frae Aberdeen,
> The best and truest ever seen;
> Nae mair shall he again proclaim
> The prophecies in *Rhymer's* name;
> Nor sell again the great commands,
> Nor praise the beuk ca'd *Meally Hands*;
> Nor *Arry's* ware for lads or lasses,
> Which for the highest wisdom passes;
> Nor shall he *Jock and Maggie's* tale
> Again expose to view or sale;
> Nae mair shall he e'er gain a dram
> Upon the tricks o' *Louden Tam*;
> *Buchanan's* wit he cannot praise,
> As aft he did in former days;
> Nor tell how *Leper* threw the cat
> Into auld Janet's boiling pat.—
>
> * * * *

[Death's] sov'reign will nae doubt it was,
Altho' we canna' tell the cause,
To drive poor Peter from the earth,
An' cause sic mourning into Perth,
Where lang the honest body dwelt,
Where mony a hunder beuk he selt,
An' where ten thousand wad defend him,
And sae wad ilk ane done that kend him.
Alas! poor Pate! nae mair will ye
Tell tales again wi' mirth and glee;
Lang will the country lasses weary,
To see that face was ay sae cheery,
A face, weel kent o'er Britain's Isle,
A face ay painted with a smile.

O wha will now fill up thy place,
And fill it with so good a grace?
There's only one that I do ken,
Amang the mortal sons o' men,
An' that is Jackey; ance thy friend,
The fittest fellow e'er I kend;
Thy customers he knew right well,
An' can a canty story tell,
On winter nights, while round the ingle,
The wheels an' reels an' plates do jingle,
So let him now tak' up the trade,
An' then I'm sure his fortune's made.

§ 6. The foregoing remarks will serve to show the nature of the packman's trade and wares, as also what were accounted the best known and most popular chap-books. Broadly speaking, these productions fall to be considered under five heads: 1, Humorous; 2, Instructive; 3, Romantic; 4, Superstitious; 5, Songs, Ballads, and Party Squibs.

(1.) CLASS I.—The Humorous subdivides into two, in the first of which some semi historical or fictitious personage is employed as a central figure round which to group a heterogeneous series of facetiæ and tales. No attempt is made to secure dramatic unity, and the pseudo-hero is generally half knave and half fool, with a dash of the philosopher when occasion demands. Scottish heroes of this kind are fairly numerous, and with them, of course, these chapters will chiefly deal; but as the exploits with which they are credited are borrowed from foreign sources, through the medium, generally, of English chap-books, brief incidental notices will be given of works which do not immediately fall within the somewhat limited province assigned to this book. The rollicking blades best known north of the Tweed are *George Buchanan, Silly Tam, John Falkirk, Leper the Tailor, John Cheap the Chapman, Lothian Tom, Wise Willie and Witty Eppie, Peter Pickup, Paddy from Cork, The Wise Men of*

Gotham, Simple John, and *Tom Tram.* As will be shown presently, the four last-mentioned are not distinctively local; but for reasons to be explained shortly, are included among the witty heroes popular on Scottish soil. Of the English rivals to these personages, *Simple Simon, Old Hobson, John Ogle, John Franky, Tom Long, Poor Robin, The Unfortunate Son and the Unfortunate Daughter, Tom Stitch, Swalpo the Pickpocket,* and *Roger the Clown,* with, perhaps, *Tarleton,* and *Taffy,* are among the best known. These somewhat rough and ready, and, by no means, exhaustive lists, so run into and merge with one another, that, in some instances, it is difficult to draw a hard and fast line between them. Thus, *Silly Tam* and *Simple John,* both Scotchmen, are almost identical with the English *Simple Simon;* and *Leper the Tailor* and *Lothian Tom* bear a strong resemblance to *Wanton Tom Stitch the Tailor;* while *Taffy* and *The Wise Men of Gotham* belong, in a literary point of view, to no particular nationality; but claim their descent from many different sources.

In two essential features, however,—the plan of construction and the general character of the incident—these histories are all alike. As to the particular quarter from which the various adventures to which they relate, are derived, it is not easy to speak definitely. This, however, is certain, that 'Ovid,' 'Gesta Romanorum,' the 'Seven Viziers,' 'Seven Sages,' 'Don Quixote,' the 'Decameron,' and most of the best-known storehouses of eastern, mediæval and classical fiction, have furnished the ideas, in some instances the exact fables, of a large proportion of the stories included in the vulgar literature of England and Scotland. To give a few out of many instances:—The judgment of the rape, attributed both to George Buchanan and Tom Tram, is borrowed from 'Sancho Panza;' Buchanan's ruse by which he contrives to be driven to London from Cornwall, when he has not so much money as will pay his hotel bill, is stolen verbatim from 'Tarleton's Jests;' while the story of the poor woman and the three mercantile swindlers is from the 'Seven Sages,' and is common among the collections of Latin tales of the thirteenth and fourteenth centuries. It is also narrated in the *Nouveaux contes à rire*, (Amsterdam, 1737,) under the title of the *Jugement subtil du duc d'Ossone contre duix Marchands*. So, also, Tom Tram's device by which he obtains £5 for preventing a man from being cuckolded, is a common mediæval tale; the popular episode, 'My Uncle's Ghost,' is from the 'Decameron;' and the story of the 'Three Wishes' is repeated in slightly varying forms in the 'Parables of Sandabar,' the 'Indian Pantcha-tautra,' the 'Seven Sages,' and the 'Confessio Amantis.' Lothian Tom's trick by which he out-wits his lawyer is but a repetition, in a modified form, of the story of old Hobson, and his servant, on their ride to Bristowe. From the 'Gesta Romanorum,' again, we have Jack Franky's expedient by which he outran his pursuer; the comical Irish bull of the three dreamers and the loaf; the proverbial three black crows; and the tragedy of the goose and the golden eggs. Probably, also, Boccaccio's story of 'Why the Gentlewoman of Lyons sat with her hair clipt off, in Purgatory,' (Giorn, VII., Nov. 6,) suggested, through the medium of *Tarleton's Newes*, (1590), the cutting off the wife's hair by the wise man of Gotham. The incident appeared originally in the *Disciplina Clericalis*, of Peter Alfonsi, and is to be found in most of the Eastern series of tales, as also in Poggius, and in many of the collections of facetiæ of the sixteenth and seventeenth centuries. What, again, are the misfortunes of *Simple John;* the beating of pots, and the losing of the mutton, by *Tom Tram;* with the various incidents narrated in *Buchaven* and the *Wise Men of Gotham:* but reproductions of the Grecian bulls perpetrated by the ever popular *skolastikos?* Finally, George Buchanan's stories of the poor tailor who accidentally killed a man; of the books and the bellows; and of the difference between a Scot and a sot: are taken *literatim* from the *Apothegms of Francis Bacon*.

But after making all allowance for this wholesale and innocent plagiarism, and acknowledging that the incidents in most of these humorous histories have been borrowed from the facetiæ of every age and country, there still remain their setting, their language, and their tone, which are distinctly and intensely original and local. Were they merely a rehash of the old fables, with which Gower, Chaucer, Boccaccio, and Shakespeare, and, in our own day, Mr. Furnival, Dr. Halliwell-Phillips, and others, have familiarised the public, they would not deserve more than a passing glance. But they are not this; for, while in many cases, the outlines are borrowed, the whole filling up, the customs narrated, the dialogue, and many of the incidents, are so essentially and characteristically Scotch, that they could not possibly have been grown on foreign soil. These rough, broad histories are saturated with an intensely local colouring, as indeed they must have been to have appealed so forcibly to the sympathies of their patrons. The incidents, though plundered from many foreign sources, have still about them a wonderful freshness and flavour, the result mainly of the manner in which they are wrought out, and the racy vernacular in which they are told.

Another and more valuable class of humorous chap-books is that in which there is a certain definite plot, accompanied by a large proportion of dialogue, and elaborated to a legitimate conclusion. Of this class, the most popular are: In prose—*Jockie and Maggie's Courtship*, and *The History of the Haverel Wives, or Janet Clinker's Orations;* and, in verse—*The Wife of Beath, Watty and Meg, The Monk and the Miller's Wife, Thrummy Cap*, and, in verse and prose—*Habby Simpson*. These furnish the choicest specimens of national humour and customs, and are replete with graphic descriptions of persons and manners. Here are three portraits of *Sawny the Coalman*, representing *Sawny* sober, *Sawny* dressed, and *Sawny* drunk.

§ 1. SAWNY SOBER.—"He was a stout young raw loun, full-faced, wi' flabby cheeks, duddy breeks, and a ragged doublet ; gade always wi' his bosom bare, sometimes had ae gartan, a lingle or rash-rape was good enough for Sawny. His very belly was a' sun-burnt, and brown like a piper's bag, or the head of an old drum ; and yet he was a ruddy loun in the face, and swallowed brose for his breakfast, and baps and ale through the day, and when the wind was cauld, bought an oven farl and twa Dunbarweathers, or a Glasgow-Magistrate, which fish-wives ca's a Weslin-herrin.

§ 2. SAWNY DRESSED.—Up got *Sawny* in the morning, and swallowed his sodden meat, slag by slag; and aff he goes to the coals and courting, lilting and singing like a lav'rock in a May morning, "O to be married if this be the way." The colliers all wondered to see him sae weal busket, with a pair of wally side auld-fashioned breeks o' his father's, and a lang gravat like a minister, or Bailie Duff at a burial, clean face and hands, and no less than a gun-sleeved linen sark on him, which made his cheeks to shine like a sherney weight, and the colliers swore he was as braw as a horse gaun to a cow's dredgy.

§ 3. SAWNY DRUNK.—When *Sawny* came out he stoited and staggered as a sturdy stot: molash was chief commander, for he thought everybody had twa heads and four een, and more noses than they needed; being sometime in the dark house, thought it was the morning of a new day. . . . Off he goes, steering about like a ship against the wind, as if he would make holes in the wa's and windows with his elbows: he looked as fierce as a lion; wi' a red face like a trumpeter, and his nose was like a bublie-cock's neb, as blue as blawirt; but or he ran half way, his head turned heavier than his heels, and mony a filthy fa' he got; thro' thick and thin he plashed, till hame he gets at last grunting and graping by the wa's, that auld Mary, his mither, thought it was their neighbour's sow, he was sae bedaubed wi' dirt."

The hand-to-hand fight that accompanied the bedding of *Jockie* and *Maggie* is also vigorously painted:

"For the hamsheughs were very great, until auld uncle Rabby came in to redd them; and a sturdy auld fallow he was. He stood stively with a stiff rumple, and by strength of his arms rave them sindry, flinging the tane east and the tither wast, until they stood a' round about like as many breathless forfoughten cocks, and no ane durst steer anither for him; Jockie's mither was driven o'er a kist, and brogit a' her hips on a round heckle. Up she gat, and rinning to fell Maggie's mither wi' the ladle, sweared she was the mither of a' the mischief that happened. Uncle Rabby ran in between them; he having a long nose, like a trumpet, she recklessly came o'er his lobster neb a drive wi' the ladle till the blood sprang out, an' ran down his auld grey beard and hang like bubles at it; O! then he gaed wood, and looked as woefu' like as he had been a tod-lowrie come frae worrying the lambs, wi' his bloody mouth. Wi' that he gets an auld flail, and rives awa' the supple, then drives them a' to the back o' the door, but yet nane wan out. Then wi' chirten' an' chappen', down comes the clayhallen and the hen bawk wi' Rab Reid, the fiddler, who had crept up aside the hens for the preservation o' his fiddle."

Few things could be more dramatic or humorous than the account of *Jockie's* interview, first with the justice, and afterwards with the minister; or *Sawny's* description of how he made love to old *Be-go's* daughter, and the exit of the little tailor 'body' with his tail between his feet, like a half-worried colly dog. Or take *Janet Clinker's* philippic against the minister's family:

"Indeed I think he (the minister) is a gay gabby body, but he ha' twa fau'ts and his wife has three; he's unco greedy o' siller, and preaching down pride and up charity, and yet he's that fu' o' pride himsel' that he has gotten a glass winnock on ilka side of his nose, and his een is as clear as twa clocks to luk' to; he has twa gilly gawkies o' dochters, wha come to the Kirk wi' their coblethow mutches frizled up as braid as their hips, and clear things like stars about their necks, and at ilka lug a wallopin white thing hanging, syne about their necks a bit thin claith like a mouse web, and their twa bits o' paps ay playing nidity nod, shining thro' like twa yearning bags. Shame fa' them and their fligmagaeries baith, for I get nae gude o' the preaching looking at them, and a' the shairney hought hizzies in the parish maun ha'e the like or lang gae. But an' I were to preach, sic pride sudna ha'e baith peace and prosperity in my parish: I wa'd point my finger at them in the Kirk and name them, baith name and surname, and say there sits shairney Meg o' the mill; stumpy May o' the Moss; sniveling Kate, with her bodle mak-easter coat; they come into the Kirk, bobbing their hint quarters like water wagtails, shaking their heads like a hunderpound horse, and what shall I compare them to?—painted Jezebels, the —— of Babylon, Rachel ——, wi' a' their gaudy decoying colours, high taps, and spread glittering tails, when they come into the house o' prayer, as it were a house of dancing and deboshery. Gae, ye painted peeswips, to fairs or waddins, and their display your proud banners o' pride; but if the gilly gawkies should come into the Kirk wi' their heels up and their heads down, our Mess John is like ane o' the dogs of Egypt, he wou'dna move his tongue, and, I believe, he darna for clippock his wife."

There is not only much humour, but a good deal of vigour and satirical power in these extracts. Indeed, vigour is characteristic of all the humorous chap-books; the metaphors in which are often as striking and straightforward as anything in Chaucer. This is the how *Sawny* felt, on wakening, after his potations with old *Be-go* the night before:

"Poor *Sawny* had a terrible nicht o't wi' a sair head and a sick heart. His een stood in his head, and he had a soughing in his lugs like a sawmill, and everything ran round him a' that day." Next day, being better. "he got his claise clean, his hair comb'd and greas'd wi' butter, and his face as clean as the cat had licked it." Even yet, however, "he was as pale as a ghost from the grave, and his face was entirely white like a weel bleached dish clout."

But if *Sawny* was ill looking, what can be said of mother *Clinker*, who was so anxious to be married, although "she look'd like the picture of death riding on hunger's back for want o' teeth to chew bread for the nourishment of the body."

§ 7. (2.) The Instructive Chap-books are so numerous as almost to defy classification; but, roughly speaking, they may be ranged under one or other of these five heads:— *a*, Historical; *b*, Biographical; *c*, Religious and Moral; *d*, Manuals of Instruction; *e*, Almanacks.

a. Most prominent among the histories is Dougal Graham's metrical account of the Rebellion of 1745-6, followed by the histories of:

"Drumclog and Bothwell Bridge,' 'The Twelve Cæsars,' 'The Kings and Queens of England and Scotland,' 'Free Masonry,' 'A New Historical Catechism,' 'The Battle of Otterburn,' 'Chevy Chase,' 'Executions in Scotland from the year 1600,' 'Massacre of Glencoe,' 'Edinburgh,' 'Glasgow Cathedral and High Church,' 'Siege of Gibraltar,' 'History of the Gentle Craft,' 'Explosion of the Prince in 1752,' 'Remarkable Earthquakes,' 'England,' 'Scotland,' 'London Plague of 1665,' 'Narrative of Four Sailors,' 'Botany Bay,' 'Crazy

Jane,' 'The Devil,' 'The Savage Girl,' 'Trial of Sir A. G. Kinloch.'

b. The Biographies include:

'Johnny Armstrong,' 'Robin Hood,' 'Wallace,' 'Bruce,' 'Black Douglas,' 'Mary Queen of Scots,' 'Napoleon Bonaparte,' 'Mahomet,' 'Jane Shore,' 'The Fair Rosamond,' 'Robert Burns,' 'Bishop Usher,' 'Enoch,' 'The Wonderful Roman Prophet,' 'Thomas the Rhymer,' 'Alexander Peden,' 'Dr. Donald,' 'John Knox,' 'Prince Charles,' 'The Rev. Dr. Cargill,' 'Robert Nixon and Bishop of Arles,' 'Dr. Van Hasn,' 'John Porter,' 'James Allan, the Northumberland Piper,' 'William Lithgow,' 'Peter Williamson;' also, accounts of 'David Haggart, the Murderer,' 'George Barnwell,' 'Paul Jones,' 'Redmond O'Hanlan,' 'Dick Turpin,' 'Murdoch Currie,' 'Rob Roy,' 'M'Pherson,' 'Fleming,' 'Gilder Roy,' 'The Irish Assassin,' 'William Burke,' 'Moll of Flanders,'—robbers and cut-throats; 'The Madrid Shaver,' 'Charles Jones,' 'Black Jack of Knaresborough,' 'Jane Arnold,' 'Bamfylde Moore Carew,' 'David Huntly,' 'Hector M'Lean,' 'Elizabeth Stewart and James Covey,' 'Mrs. Johnston, the Captive American,' and 'Jean of Bogmoor.'

c. Not less numerous are the Religious and Moral Chap-books, among which are:

'A Choice Drop of Honey,' 'Sins and Sorrows,' 'A Token for Mourners,' 'The Plant of Renown,' 'A Prayer Book,' 'The New Pictorial Bible,' 'The Pilgrim's Progress,' 'A Wedding Ring,' 'Judas Iscariot,' 'Moses,' 'Joseph and Paul,' 'Abraham,'

'Isaac,' 'Jacob and Jonah,' 'Female Policy, or Designing Women,' 'The Wonderful Advantages of Drunkenness,' Allan Ramsay's 'Scotch Proverbs,' 'Betsy Brown,' 'The Afflicted Parent,' 'The London Spy,' 'Honesty in Distress,' 'Richard's Maxims,' 'The Shepherd of Salisbury Plain.'

d. The long list of Manuals of Instruction comprises:

'The Housekeeper,' 'The Cookery Book,' 'The Way to Wealth,' 'The Valentine Writer,' 'The Polite Letter Writer,' 'The Book of Etiquette,' 'The Vermin Killer,' 'Money-Catching,' 'Franklin's Art of Swimming,' 'Description of the Emperor of China's Palace,' 'The Angler's Guide,' 'The Freemason's Catechism,' and 'Almanacks,' the almost infinite variety and number of which defy enumeration.

It is not necessary to give any farther account of the larger portion of the books above mentioned. The purely historical narratives are simply written, and generally accurate as to matters of fact; and as they may be had at most book-sellers at the present moment, they need not detain us longer.

§ 8. (3.) ROMANTIC.—Of the Romances and Fairy Tales, the following are, perhaps, the best known:

'Beauty and the Beast,' 'Whittington and his Cat,' 'Jack the Giant Killer,' 'Jack and the Bean

Stalk,' 'Tom Thumb,' 'Ali Baba and the Forty Thieves,' 'Aladdin and the Wonderful Lamp,' 'Sinbad the Sailor,' 'Prince Lupin,' 'Valentine and Orson,' 'Cinderella,' 'Blue Beard,' 'Robin Hood,' 'The Babes in the Wood,' 'The Babes in the Wood, Continued,' 'Dorastus and Fawnia,' 'The Young Robber,' 'Puss in Boots,' 'Gulliver's Travels,' 'Robinson Crusoe,' 'Sixteen-Fingered Jack,' 'The Little White Mouse,' 'Æsop's Fables,' 'The Sleeping Beauty of the Wood,' 'The White Fawn,' 'Thomas Hickathrift,' 'Hero and Leander,' 'The Seven Champions,' 'The Wild Huntsman,' 'The Bitter Wedding,' 'The Long Pack,' 'The Ghost of My Uncle,' 'Tragedy of the Perjured Bride,' 'The Bewitched Fiddler;' 'Baron Munchausen,' 'The Two Drovers,' 'The Countess of Essex,'—the last of which has furnished the plot of Mr. Tennyson's ballad of Lord Burleigh,—'Jack Horner,' 'St. George,' 'The Shepherdess of the Alps,' 'Sir Gawen and the Enchanted Castle,' 'The Cruel Baron of Normandine,' 'History of the Gentle Craft,' 'The Triumph of Love,' 'The Wonderful Adventures of Sixteen Seamen,' 'Baron Trenck,' 'The Wandering Jew,' 'The Cottage Wedding,' 'Roderick Random,' 'Don Quixote,' 'Dr. Faustus,' 'The King and the Cobler,' 'The King and the Miller of Mainsfield,' 'Siege of Troy,' 'The Iron Shroud,' 'Constant Jenny and Nancy,' 'The Spectre Bridegroom,' 'The Maid and the Magpie,' 'The Old Woman and Her Silver Penny,' 'The Fairy and the Fish,' 'Tom the Piper's Son,' 'Tom Tucker,' 'The Butterfly's Ball,' 'John Gilpin,' 'Old Dame Trot,' 'Cock Robin,' 'The Little Old Woman and the Peddler,' 'Mother

Hubbard,' 'The House that Jack Built,' 'Goody Two Shoes,' 'The Misfortunes of Toby Tickle-Pitcher,' 'Duncan Campbell and His Dog Oscar,' 'Mansie Wauch,' 'The Broken Heart,' and 'The Village Curate.'

With the exception of *Blind Allan*, by Wilson, the *Two Drovers*, by Hogg, the Ettrick Shepherd, *Mansie Wauch*, and *Duncan Campbell*, none of the above are distinctively Scottish, and are, besides, too well known to require criticism.

§ 9. (4). SUPERSTITIOUS.—This class is one of great interest and even historical importance, and, in the event of another edition, will be treated at length. The best known works that fall under this catalogue are:

'Visits to the World of Spirits,' 'Mother Bunch's Fortune-teller,' 'Napoleon's Book of Fate,' 'The Prophecies of Thomas a' Rhymer, Peden, Bede, Usher, Enoch, Dr. Donald, Bishop of Arles, Van Hasn, Nixon, Mrs. Shipton, Porter, Christopher Love, and Rev. Allan Logan, of Culross,' 'The Conjuror's Guide,' 'The Golden Dreamer,' 'The Spaewife,' 'The Fortune-teller,' 'Satan's Invisible World Discovered,' 'The Laird of Coole's Ghost,' 'Sir R. Grierson of Lag,' 'The Magic Oracle,' 'The Royal Dreamer,' 'The Mole Interpreter,' 'Maggy Bell,' 'History of the Devil,' 'Judas Iscariot,' 'The Wandering Jew,' 'History of Dreams,'

'A Wonderful Trance,' 'Davis the Dream-interpreter.'

The foregoing, with the songs and ballads, comprise the main bulk of the chap-books which at one time or another have been widely circulated north of the Tweed. Of late years, a change has come over this sort of literature, by the wholesale introduction of a very low and very sensational type of fiction, in the shape of penny and twopenny novels. As these, however, do not fall within the scope of this work, and are, besides, of very recent date, an enumeration of the titles of a few, which have been issued by a Glasgow publisher, will suffice:

'The Rebel Spy, or The King's Volunteers;' a Romance of the Siege of Boston. 'The Renegade, or The Secrets of the Gulf Mill;' a Story of the Shores and Waters of Connecticut. 'The Vow of Revenge,' a Tale of Love and the Triumph of Innocence. 'The Mysterious Protector,' a Tale of Plot and Passion. 'The Gold Digger of California,' or The Mysterious Miner.' 'Julia St. Clair, or The Angel of the Wilderness.' 'The Stolen Beauty of the Rio Grande.' 'The Lovers' Trials, or The Bridal at Last.' 'Clara's Rescue, or Ned Wentworth's Vow.' 'The Rivals, or The Secret Shot.' 'Romance of The Texan Pampas, or The Hermit of the Colorado Hills.' 'The Gold Seeker's Daughter, or The

Dream Realized.' 'The Flight for Life, or Long Bill the Trapper.' 'The Treasure Cave, or The Buccaneer's Secret.' 'The Trial of the Redskins,' a Romance of The White Pine District; and 'Dick Raymonds Claim, or The King of the Borderman.'

§ 10. The history and authorship of the chap-books now fall to be discussed. It would, of course, be useless to attempt to trace such works as *Jack the Giant Killer*, and the long series of nursery tales, to their origin. To do so would require not a chapter but a volume, and it would be presumption to follow in the steps of so able and erudite an investigator as Mr. Thomas Keightly. All that can be done in this chapter is to take the works which are supposed to be, or actually are, of native origin and growth, and attempt to track them to their respective sources. Of these, the principal are comprised in the following list:

'George Buchanan,' 'Lothian Tom,' 'John Cheap,' 'Leper the Tailor,' 'John Falkirk,' 'Paddy from Cork,' 'Tom Tram,' 'Simple John,' ('Silly Tam'), 'The History of Buchaven,' 'Jockie and Maggie's Courtship,' 'The Coalman's Courtship,' 'Janet Clinker's Orations,' 'The History of the Haverel Wives,' 'The Wife of Beath,' 'Watty and Meg,' 'Thrummy

Cap,' 'The Goodwife and the Minister,' 'The Dominie Deposed,' 'The Magic Pill, or Davie and Bess,' 'The Pleasures of Matrimony,' 'A Diverting Courtship,' 'The Art of Courtship,' 'The Grand Solemnity of the Tailor's Funeral,' 'Alexander Hamwinkle,' 'Sir John Barleycorn,' 'Copy of a Letter from a Young-Shepherd,' 'A Warning to the Methodist Preacher,' 'A Second Warning to the Methodist Preacher,' 'John Falkirk's Cariches,' 'Peter Pickup,' 'The Monk and the Miller's Wife,' 'The Long Pack,' 'My Uncle's Ghost,' 'Grierson of Lag,' 'The World of Invisible Spirits,' 'Habby Simpson,' and 'Mansie Wauch :' besides several slighter prose sketches, printed on broad-sheets.

By far the most important of these have been attributed to the pen of Dougal Graham, to whom reference has been already made, and who wrote most of his works between 1745 and 1779. The external evidence on the subject is somewhat conflicting and unsatisfactory, and is based on the following authorities:

1. William Motherwell, the poet;
2. John McVean, the bibliopole of the Highstreet, and editor of McUre's 'History of Glasgow;'
3. Doctor Strang, author of 'Glasgow and its Clubs;'

to which might almost be added the late Mr. Alexander Strathern, for many years sheriff-substitute in Glasgow, and well known in local circles for his antiquarian tastes.

1. William Motherwell, the poet, in his article on chap-books, in the *Paisley Magazine* for 1824, ascribes the following works, without hesitation, to Dougal Graham.

1. Jockie and Maggie, five parts, 1783.
2. Paddy from Cork, 1784.
3. Lothian Tom, six parts, 1793.
4. John Cheap, three parts, 1786.
5. John Falkirk, 1779.
6. John Falkirk's Cariches.
7. Janet Clinker's Orations.

The three last, he explains, were often printed together, the *Orations* being sometimes issued separately under the title of *Grannie McNab's Lectures to the Society of Clashing Wives, Glasgow, &c.*

8. Leper the Tailor, Part I. and II., 1779.
9. Simple John and his Twelve Misfortunes.

As to the authorship of these nine, Motherwell speaks with perfect confidence, as of a well-established and universally admitted fact. He also adds, that he should not be surprised to learn that Graham was also the author of 'George Buchanan,' 'The Coalman's Courtship,' and 'The History of

Buchaven,' and challenges anyone to produce an edition of one or other of these works of a date prior to the era in which Graham flourished.

2. A foot-note to Dr. Strang's account of Dougal Graham contains the following:

"In a manuscript of the late Mr. McVean, the antiquarian bibliopole of the High street, we find the following list of the *Opera Dugaldi*, so far as he had met with them, keeping out of view his lyrical productions, which were very numerous:—

1. George Buchanan, six parts.
2. Paddy from Cork, three parts.
3. Leper the Tailor, two parts.
4. John Falkirk, the Merry Piper.
5. Janet Clinker's Oration on the Virtues of the Old and the Pride of Young Women.
6. John Falkirk's Curiosities (*sic*), five parts.
7. John Cheap the Chapman, three parts.
8. Lothian Tom, six parts.
9. The History of Buchaven, with cuts.
10. Jockie and Maggie's Courtship, five parts.
11. The Follower (*sic*) of Witless Women; or, the History of the Haverel Wives.
12. The Young Creelman's (*sic*) Courtship to a Creelwife's daughter, two parts.
13. Simple John and his Twelve Misfortunes.
14. The Grand Solemnity of the Tailor's Funeral, who lay nine days in state on his own shopboard; together with his last will.

15. The Remarkable Life and Transactions of Alexander Hamwinkle, Heckler, Dancing-master, and Ale-seller in Glasgow, now banished for coining.
16. The Dying Groans of Sir John Barleycorn, being his grievous complaint against the brewers of bad ale; to which is added Donald Drouth's reply, with a large description of his Drunken Wife.
17. A Warning to the Methodist Preachers.
18. A Second Warning to the Methodist Preachers.

3. Dr. Strang's personal evidence is brief:

"Of the vulgar literature to which we have referred, and of so much of which Dougal Graham was the author, it is enough to say that it constituted the chief literary pabulum enjoyed by the bulk of our countrymen in the humbler walks of life; and though the jokes therein promulgated certainly were broad, and sometimes even grossly indecent, they were not untrue portraits of Scottish life and Scottish manners. By means of the numerous merchant peddlers who, in those days of bad roads and worse conveyances, perambulated the country, these cheap stories of Dougal Graham were introduced into every cottage where any of the dealers rested for a night, or were disposed of by them at any country fair which they might chance to visit; hence the exploits of 'George Buchanan,' the histories of 'John Cheap the Chapman,' 'Leper the Tailor,' 'Lothian Tom,' 'Simple John and his Twelve Misfortunes,' and such like, although all saturated with indecency, formed the chief materials of the peasant's library; the which, notwithstanding all that has been said about the moral and religious character of the country people, proves how much the national humor and peculiarities of the humbler classes of the Scottish population were then, as we believe they still are considerably, imbued with coarseness and indelicacy."

4. The late Mr. Sheriff Strathern, in a paper read before the Glasgow Archæological Society, 6th April, 1863, writes as follows:

"It is difficult to give them in order of publication, but I have, at some little trouble, collected a few of the editions, and, as near as I can reach it, this is the order in which the works appeared. His earliest was 'The Whole Proceedings of Jockie and Maggie,' in five parts, published in 1783. The table of contents, and more so the book itself, are not for ears polite; although there is throughout a large share of rough jokes, pungent, coarse wit, and droll invective. This is one of Dugald's best productions, and has run through numerous editions. 'The Comical Sayings of Paddy from Cork,' followed, and was printed for George Caldwell, Paisley, in 1784. Then 'The History and Comical Transactions of Lothian Tom' succeeded. But successful as this proved, it was eclipsed by the 'History of John Cheap the Chapman: containing above a hundred merry exploits done by him and his traveller Drouthy Tam, a Sticket Weaver.' 'The Comical and Witty Jokes of John Falkirk the

Merry Piper, when in courtship to an old fiddler's widow who wanted the teeth,' followed; and, as a sequel, Dugald afterwards issued 'The Scots Piper's Queries; or John Falkirk's caritches for the trial of dull wits and instruction of ignorant people.' But his greatest achievement was 'Fun upon Fun, or the Comical Tricks of Leper the Tailor;' which he announced as printed for the flying stationers in town and country. 'Janet Clinker's Oration on the Virtues of Old Women and the Pride of the Young' was published without date; and it was shortly followed by 'Grannie McNab's Lecture on the Society of Clashing Wives, (Glasgow); or Witless Mothers and Dandy Daughters who bring them up to hoodwink the men and deceive them with their braw dresses, when they can neither wash a sark, mak parritch, or gang to the well.' The last authentic production of Dugald's which I have ever seen was the 'Comical History of Simple John and his Twelve Misfortunes;' giving a particular account of his courtship and marriage to a scolding wife, which has been a mortifying misery to many a poor man.' Fame has attributed some others to Dugald, such as: 'the Merry Exploits of George Buchanan,' the 'Creelman's Courtship,' and the 'History of Buckhaven, containing the witty and entertaining exploits of Wise Willie and Witty Eppy;' but I have seen the authority of these controverted."

The above exhausts the external evidence on the point: there still remains the internal evidence, that is, the testimony furnished by the works themselves, which is extremely meagre. In the preface to an early edition of *John Falkirk's Cariches*—John Falkirk being a nickname sometimes applied to Graham—*Falkirk,* the witty Scot's Piper, is reported to have written "many small tracts, and the following curious and diverting pieces are said to be of his composition, viz.: *The History of John Cheap the Chapman, The History of the Haverel Wives, Janet Clinker's Orations, John Falkirk's Witty Jokes, Jockie and Maggie's Courtship, The Proverbs of the Pride of Women, History of Lothian Tom,* with many others, which are well known in Scotland, England, and Ireland."

From the above it will be seen that the only two authorities deserving attention are Motherwell and McVean. Dr. Strang seems to have copied the accounts of Graham given by these two writers, and Mr. Sheriff Strathern confined himself to reproducing Strang and Motherwell; the list of editions which he "collected at some little trouble" being all but identical with the Paisley poet's. The value of the evidence of the introductory to *John Falkirk's Cariches* is merely traditional, the preface having been written after Graham's death. Neither is Mr. McVean's list quite satisfactory; and at least three of the titles are incorrectly given: *John Falkirk's Cariches* being transformed into *Curiosities*; *The Follies of Witless Women* into *The Follower of Witless Women;* and *The Young Coalman's Courtship* into the *Young Creelman's Courtship*. These mistakes, of course, may have resulted from the carelessness of the person who copied Mr. McVean's list; at any rate, their presence is unsatisfactory. But these are venial slips compared with the insertion in the list, without a word of explanation, of *George Buchanan, The History of Buchaven,* and *Simple John*. Judging from internal evidence, it is extremely improbable that Graham ever composed the two first of these, and it is absolutely certain that he did not write the last. The original hero of the 'Misfortunes' is *Simple Simon;* a history of whose life and misadventures was common in England in the seventeenth century. This, or a similar version—most likely one of the many editions issued from Newcastle—Graham most certainly stole, and, having changed the hero's name to *John*, and written a racy introduction to the work in board Scotch, gave it to the world as an original production. The prefatory matter is quite in Graham's style, and could not have been written by an Englishman. It is frequently to be found published separately under the title of *Silly Tam*. As to *George Buchanan* and *Buchaven*, they may have been sold to the publishers by Dougal as his own composition; but there is not a single sentence in either of them that might not have been written by any one else; and most of the incidents narrated were to be found in the facetiæ of almost every country in Europe ages before Graham carried a pack or rang the skellat bell of Glasgow. Remarks of a like nature apply, also, to *Paddy from Cork*, although this is less of a compilation, and has more local colouring than the three already named. There still remains for consideration the article by William Motherwell, which, although conspicuously inaccurate in certain details, furnishes quite the best evidence now existing on the subject; only one change being necessary to make his list, so far as it goes, correct—namely, the substitution of *Coalman's Courtship* and *Silly Tam*, for *Paddy from Cork* and *Simple John*. Motherwell merely hazards a guess that the *Coalman* is one of Graham's progeny; but no competent judge, or expert in style, who compares that work with *Jockie and Maggie* and *Janet Clinker's Orations*, can reasonably doubt that to Graham, and to Graham alone, belongs the credit of the composition. The following lists include as many of Graham's works as are either known or supposed to be his:

1. *The Works of Dougal Graham.*

1. The Metrical History of the Rebellion of 1745–6.
2. Jockie and Maggie, five parts.
3. Lothian Tom, six parts.
4. John Cheap, three parts.
5. Janet Clinker's Orations, or Grannie McNab's Lectures.
6. Leper the Tailor, two parts.
7. The Grand Solemnity of the Tailor's Funeral, (probably part three of Leper the Tailor).

8. The Coalman's Courtship.
9. Simple Tam, *alias* Simple John, (being the introduction to the Twelve Misfortunes).
10. Turnamspike.
11. John Hielandman.
12. Proverbs on the Pride of Women.
13. The History of the Haverel Wives.

.2 *Works Probably Written by Graham.*

14. Verses entitled 'Dugald McTaggart.'
15. Verses on the Popular Superstitions of Scotland.
16. Rhythmical Dialogue between the Pope and the Devil.
17. An Epitaph on the Third Commandment.
18. The Remarkable Life and Transactions of Alexander Hamwinkle.
19. A Warning to the Methodist Preachers.
20. A Second Warning to the Methodist Preachers.

3. *Works Compiled or Edited by Graham.*

21. Paddy from Cork, three parts.
22. Simple John and his Twelve Misfortunes, (partly included in No. 9).
23. John Falkirk.
24. John Falkirk's Cariches.

4. *Works Attributed to Graham.*

25. The Dying Groans of Sir John Barleycorn.
26. The History of Buchaven.
27. Verses on the Pride of Women.

Of the remaining chap-books,—with the exception of *Watty and Meg, The Pleasures of Matrimony, Blind Allan, Mansie Wauch, The Dominie Deposed, The Monk and the Miller's Wife, Satan's Invisible World of Spirits* and the *Tinklarian Tracts*,—almost nothing is known as to their authorship. Even of Graham's productions it is impossible to ascertain the exact order of publication. Motherwell's list is almost our only guide, and except Part II. of *Leper the Tailor*, none of the editions mentioned by him were the original. This only can be said, that they were all issued as nearly as possible between 1745 and 1779, and they contribute the most important and characteristic portion of the popular literature of Scotland. Yet, in spite of their good points, their genuine humour, their historical worth, and the fact that for more than half a century they were the most popular and almost the sole literary entertainment of the humbler ranks in Scotland, and latterly in the north of England and parts of Ireland, there is, perhaps, not one in a thousand, even of Scotchmen, who has ever thought to inquire after their history, or the life and character of their author.

So far back as 1824, Motherwell could write: "There is not a peddler who traverses broad Scotland with a pack on his back and an ell-wand in his hand, but in all likelihood disposes of some of Dougal Graham's works at every cottage he rests in for the night, or at every country fair he visits in the course of his peregrinations. When he retails the adventures of *John Cheap the Chapman, Leper the Tailor, John Falkirk's Cariches, Granny McNab's Lectures to Clashing Wives and Witless Dochters, Simple John and his Twelve Misfortunes*, every one enough to break the heart of a giant,—or the whole proceedings of *Jockie and Maggie's Courtship*,—does he bestow one thought on their humorous author?" The peddler still exists, though shorn of his old importance and dignity, and at remote country fairs the curious may even now pick up a stray copy of *Leper the Tailor* or *Lothian Tom*, but to the great bulk of the community these redoubtable heroes are quite unknown, while the very name of the once 'skellat bellman' of Glasgow, who wrote so many of these once famous histories, has clean passed from the mind of all save a few local antiquarians. This should not be so; and from the scanty records of Dougal Graham's history that survive, in tradition and printed,—but comparatively inaccessible writings,—the meagre but reliable sketch that follows in Chapter third has been composed.

www.ingramcontent.com/pod-product-compliance
Lightning Source LLC
Chambersburg PA
CBHW030253170426
43202CB00009B/723